Hello, Cutie!

ADVENTURES IN CUTE CULTURE

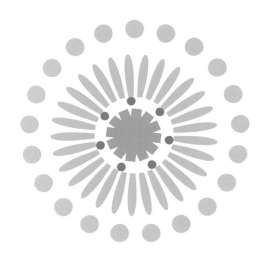

Hello, Cutie!

ADVENTURES IN CUTE CULTURE

Pamela Klaffke

ARSENAL
PULP PRESS

VANCOUVER

ARSENAL PULP PRESS
Suite 101 – 211 East Georgia St.
Vancouver, BC V6A 1Z6
Canada
arsenalpulp.com

The publisher gratefully acknowledges the support of the Canada Council for the Arts and the British Columbia Arts Council for its publishing program, and the Government of Canada (through the Canada Book Fund) and the Government of British Columbia (through the Book Publishing Tax Credit Program) for its publishing activities.

Book design by Li Eng-Lodge, Electra Design
Editing by Susan Safyan
Cover photograph by Pamela Klaffke
Author photograph by Emma Klaffke
All photographs by Pamela Klaffke unless otherwise noted

Printed and bound in Canada

Library and Archives Canada Cataloguing in Publication

 Klaffke, Pamela, 1970-
      Hello cutie! : adventures in cutie culture / Pamela Klaffke.

 Includes index.
Also issued in electronic format.
ISBN 978-1-55152-472-6

      1. Collectors and collecting. I. Title.

AM501.C88K53 2012   790.1'32   C2012-903263-8

For Emma

Contents

Acknowledgments

There are so many people without whom this book would not have been possible. The staff at Arsenal Pulp Press are always a pleasure to work with, and special thanks go out to publisher Brian Lam and editor Susan Safyan for their tireless work, support of, and enthusiasm for *Hello, Cutie!* Thanks also to Carolyn Swayze and Kris Rothstein at the Swayze Literary Agency.

It's the voices in this book that really bring it to life, and I would be remiss not to thank all of the people who so generously took the time to speak with me about their experiences and share their expertise. So, big thanks to Katie Barker, Megan Besmirched, Julia Chibatar, Anna Collver, Kimberly Cook, Sara Doane, Leslie Dotson Van Every, Cynthia Flores, Meg Frost, Patrick Galbraith, Gina Garan, Mab Graves, Shimrit Hamsi, Faythe Levine, Rosanna Mackney, Toni Morberg, Missy Munday, Meghan Murphy, Christopher Noxon, Naomi Owen, Jane Pierrepont, Claire Rowlands, Crystal Scott, Victoria Suzanne, Alexandra Tyler, Crystal Watanabe, Susan Wilson, and Fanny Zara.

Hello, Cutie! was written and photographed on a particularly tight deadline, and I'm grateful to all of my family and friends who helped me out, even when that help meant indulging my crazy rants when things got tough. (Yes, Alan Duffy, Mark O'Flaherty, and Karen Powell—I'm talking about you!) My friend Masashi Kasaki was a great resource in researching this book, helping me understand Japanese customs and traditions, and kindly translating text for me. And I do have to mention Tim Hendrickson and David Bransby-Williams, pals and proprietors of my neighborhood wine shop, Wine Ink, who poured me many, much-needed glasses throughout the process.

Thanks to my parents, Rena and Richard, and to my brother, Brad, for their support and putting in extra babysitting hours. My dad, especially, deserves to have his contribution to my enduring love of cute acknowledged. The business trips to Asia he took (and the adorable gifts he always brought back) when I was a child fueled my love of cute and introduced me to the Japanese aesthetic I remain fascinated with to this day.

Thank you, too, to my partner, Gillman Payette, for his unconditional support and for shouldering much of the around-the-house duties and doing the school runs while I worked (and for volunteering himself as a handy photo assistant). And last, but by no means least, a great big thank you to my daughter, Emma, whose love of cute is infectious and reminds me every day that there's still a kid in every one of us grown-ups.

Note: I use analogue cameras and expired film for all of my professional photography work. My photographs often feature grain and blur; I like the warmth and texture, vivid color, unpredictability, and imperfection of working with film. This vintage-inspired style really lent itself well to this project, as most of the items I shot for the book are vintage, as are the fabric backdrops.

The New Cute

I'm standing on a footstool dusting a shiny pink plastic Easter basket filled with Japanese-made vintage doll heads, all sporting 1960s bouffant hairdos. The basket is perched atop a bookshelf in my living room. I take one head out and carefully run a cloth over it until I'm satisfied that it's in tip-top shape. I repeat this with another dozen or so heads, before moving on to the cluster of '70s toy clowns that are interspersed between various DVDs and books. Then it's time for the fuzzy, flocked bunnies that live beside the dual turntables under the front window, the tarted-up, stockinette pose dolls in voluminous lace gowns, and the gigantic bright blue origami bird that my fiancé remarkably fashioned from a stiff piece of poster board.

Dusting days are the worst—just ask any cute-hunter. Odd shapes, wobbly parts, and retro plastics that double as lint magnets make cleaning a challenge, but for some reason, it's all worth it. The bright colors, shiny surfaces, and smiling faces are impossible for us to resist, and while others may find our aesthetic preference for all things cute eccentric, we wouldn't have it any other way. Like so many fellow collectors I've met in my decades-long quest for cute, I've never been one for convention. Trends and fashion come and go, but I like what I like, and often find myself asking or analyzing why. I like a dash of whimsy and a whole lot of kitsch. From clothing to décor, I mix vintage with handmade with a handful of classics. I sew and I cook and play big-headed dolly games with my eleven-year-old daughter, Emma. I write stories and shoot film with old cameras. I haunt thrift shops and am always— *always*—on the prowl for the next, greatest, most absolutely cutest thing.

In recent years, it's become increasingly clear that I'm not the only one craving cute. The evidence is everywhere. Demand for the vintage cutesy-kitsch I could once pick up dirt-cheap in charity shops and online has

Plastic deer, Japan, 1960s

Hello, Cutie!

grown along with the prices. That weird, wind-up pink poodle that was made in Japan circa 1960-something? Or the sweet little lamb squeaky toy? Better snap it up now—it'll be sold to another shopper within the hour. Craft fairs and online markets are teeming with handmade cute, while notoriously cute big-name re-brands like Care Bears and Strawberry Shortcake line the shelves of big-box toy stores.

Perhaps tough economic times and social instability have us looking for relief, a cheery break from our work-a-day grind. It makes sense when you think about it; whether we're conscious of it or not, in a consumerist society it's natural to turn to objects for comfort. Modern history has taught us that this is particularly so during down and depressing times.

Just look at Japan's impressive output of exports during the mid-twentieth century. After war left the country with an unstable economy and record unemployment, Japan's dark days were short-lived. Thanks to clever government trade policies and a helping hand from the United States, Japan's economy bloomed and flourished from the mid-1950s and throughout the '60s. The turnaround was so dramatic that it earned its own title: the Japanese post-war economic miracle. While it doesn't quite roll eloquently off the tongue, the name pretty much says it all.

Barbamama PVC figurine, China, 2006, ©AT & Kodansha

Manufacturing and international trade was at the core of the miracle, and it doesn't take a lot of research time before all of the beloved made-in-Japan vintage that sits on and around my workspace is framed in a new and different light. The Japanese toys and novelties industries pushed out a mind-boggling variety of products during a boom that lasted decades, eventually morphing into a bubble economy that burst in 1991, plunging the country into an economic depression that lasted nearly ten years.

Most curious in this history lesson is those years of economic depression. When Japan was hit the last time around, after World War II, it was the likes of Osamu Tezuka's groundbreaking—and super-cute—*manga* series *Astro Boy* that pushed cute culture to the fore.

In the 1990s, it was Hello Kitty that became the worldwide symbol of cute when the character—who was created in the 1970s—experienced a phenomenal renaissance that drove the little cat to the height of its popularity and turned the company behind the cute, Sanrio, into a billion-dollar business. Astro Boy and Hello Kitty are two of the biggest names to break out of Japan's recessions, but by no means the only cuties to thrive during difficult times. Perhaps the same socio-economic forces are at play now, making cute more appealing than ever. Maybe global crisis equals cute culture surge. It's not as outrageous an idea as some may think.

Take, for example, the Great Depression that started in 1929 and lasted more than a decade. It's not a time generally associated with fun or cute or really anything good at all, but take a closer look at the culture of the time and you might be surprised at what you find. The world economy fell out just as the Golden Age of Hollywood cinema was finding its footing, and rather than shrinking, audiences swelled, new theaters were built—audiences were looking to escape and be entertained. Blues and jazz music ruled; Louis Armstrong and Duke Ellington were kings. In New York City, three icons of modern architecture were completed: the Chrysler Building, the Empire State Building, and Rockefeller Center. Then-fledgling visual artists Willem de Kooning and Jackson Pollock earned a paycheck by painting murals in government buildings. Money may have been in short supply, but creativity, art, and design certainly were not.

Nor was cute. Shirley Temple, arguably the cutest, most saccharine-sweet child actress of all time, was the number-one draw at the box office from 1935 to 1938. Playtime favorites since 1913, Kewpie dolls held strong during the Great Depression, as did cute tin plates and tea sets decorated with lithographs of nursery rhyme characters and baby animals. Not surprisingly, there was also a whole lot of adorable DIY crafting going on with moms and daughters stitching up rag dolls and teddy bears.

People congregated at shows and theaters and gathered around kitchen tables to play Monopoly—an instant hit upon its introduction in 1934—and other board games. If escapism was one constant for people of the time, another had to be the desire for unity and shared experience. Collective hardship and strife spurs a need for connection, the result of which we now witness every day online in forums, chat rooms, and the scrolling comments sections of high-traffic blogs. Economic unrest and an uncertain future, escape and connection, handmade crafts—more than eighty years after the start of the

Great Depression it would seem that history is once again doing its thing and repeating itself, only this time around the escapism, the connection, and even the handmade crafts can be found all in one place.

The Internet is without a doubt the most convenient way to share the cute, and one of the biggest enablers of cute addicts like myself is the largest handmade and vintage marketplace online, *etsy.com*. It's hard for me to imagine a life without Etsy. Most days I'm not buying, but simply browsing through pages of cute stuff, clicking on vintage dolls and admiring handmade stuffies and clothing. I sell, too, sharing my other dominant life obsession—vintage textiles and sewing ephemera—with like-minded shoppers. But every morning, after I check in with my shop, add listings, and respond to messages, I treat myself to a virtual tour of all the latest and greatest additions to Etsy. I start with vintage Japanese dolls and toys, then scour the listings for old toy catalogs and magazines, and finally move on to creepy-cute anthropomorphic playthings and *tchotchkes*. Sometimes, I'll spice things up (and add to my procrastination time) by clicking through whimsical themes like all-pink handmade plush poodles or searching exclusively for kitschy-cute inflatable toys from the 1960s. And chances are that if there is a particular item I need as a prop or accessory for a photo shoot or a specific piece I'm dying

Handmade needle-felted bunny, USA, 2010, ©Kelley Zdziarski, Little Elf's Toy Shop

to add to my pose doll collection, I will find it on Etsy.

The resurgence of handmade-everything was already in full swing and speeding towards the mainstream when Etsy launched in mid-2005. Artists and artisans, crafters and designers, vintage dealers and supplies merchants could set up shop without a lot of hassle or exorbitant fees. They came in droves, and so did the buyers. Today, Etsy hosts almost one million individual shops; sales in 2011 topped $525 million USD. The site has made handmade and vintage more accessible than ever

Handknit plush bear, 1970s

Hello, Cutie!

before, and what's good for the handmade and vintage markets is good for cute hunters. Sewing, knitting, crafting, and crochet— these are not the dirty words they once were. Hitting my teen years in the early 1980s, I often hid the fact that not only did I sew, I liked it—a lot. Making your own clothes or altering vintage pieces was considered geeky and very uncool. Three decades later, it seems there's hardly anything cooler than knowing your way around a sewing machine or a pair of knitting needles. The rise of handmade culture has been swift and Etsy's impact significant. I decide—on a lark—to type the word cute into the Etsy search box and 378,750 items come up. While everyone has their own interpretation of cute, it's clear that what's cute to so many fits nicely into the new DIY aesthetic.

But calling today's popular DIY aesthetic "new" is a bit of a misnomer, since the cute-as-can-possibly-be look is frequently and heavily influenced by vintage toys and handicrafts of the mid-twentieth century. A notable example is the crocheted stuffed toys known as *amigurumi*, and it's no surprise that the style has its roots in Japan, likely influenced by the Chinese who have been crocheting for centuries.

I had brushes with amigurumi years before I knew its name (which, translated from the Japanese, literally means crocheted or knitted stuffed doll). There's a long tradition of sewing, knitting, and crocheting in the western Canadian prairie provinces. When immigrant settlers came seeking free land, a fresh start, and a new life in the first half of the 1900s, many didn't have much and thus the domestic arts of sewing, knitting, and crochet were widely practiced. What does that mean in regards to cute? To amigurumi?

It means that the area is teeming with vintage handicrafts, patterns for handicrafts, and materials to make those handicrafts—like amigurumi. Crocheted or knitted toys were not uncommon, and through the years I've collected several handmade pieces, including two crocheted "Care Bears" and my favorite, Caramel, a beige knitted teddy bear with a round belly and a simple smile that makes it impossible not to adore him.

Japanese and Japanese-inspired amigurumi are typically much smaller than my cherished vintage friends, who stand over a foot tall. Many of today's amigurumi measure around four inches and fit snugly in the palm of one's hand. There are books—so many books!— devoted to patterns, and online you'll find countless variations of owls, dogs, and kitties, all amigurumi-style.

Amigurumi artists and their cute-crafting contemporaries have played an important role in encouraging others to learn new DIY skills. They answer questions and respond to comments on their blogs and Flickr accounts

Bun-Bun Bunny, 2011. Handmade by the author using vintage materials

Hello, Cutie!

and on their Twitter and Facebook feeds; they get to know their customers not necessarily face-to-face, but definitely one-to-one. Making money in cute culture is far from a strictly business endeavor.

Since the early days of the web—when text-driven bulletin boards were a marvel of communication, and if you had e-mail, it was a numbered Compuserve account—there were pundits stamping their feet decrying this newfangled technology, labeling it cold and dangerous and bringing us one step closer to a soulless society. These types are, of course, still around, still spouting the same rhetoric. If they are to be believed, the Internet is to blame for everything from political apathy to teens' poor spelling to the devolution of interpersonal relationships. Clearly, they are not into cute.

For hobbyists of all stripes, the Internet has been a boon. People with common interests in far-flung places could at last communicate— congregate—with ease and abandon. The online experience of meeting, chatting, buying, and selling doesn't replace our families of "real-life" friends, but it does add something to our lives that used to be so hard to find. There were days, not so very long ago, that newsletters mailed through the post were one of the only ways to communicate with fellow enthusiasts. Sometimes, there would be a special sale or fair where you could meet in person, though these events were rare and often too broad in scope. There may even have been people into just the same cute things you were, living in the same city, but how would you know? Thankfully, the Internet makes everything a small world for cute connoisseurs.

I've always been more of a lurker than a poster when it comes to online forums. I like to follow the conversation, but become strangely introverted when it comes to the prospect of posting a question or reply. When I was pregnant with my daughter and experiencing horrible morning sickness and later, bed rest, I turned to online forums in search of any hints and tips I could find. I followed the dramas that inevitably erupted between rival soon-to-be moms, but never typed a single word. It happened again when I started organizing my vintage fashion magazine collection. This time, I wasn't quite so timid and would actually ask an occasional question or contribute to a thread. It's happened most recently in regard to my collection of big-eyed Japanese and Korean dolls like Dal and Blythe.

There is a lot more to learn about these dolls than I could ever have anticipated, so I Googled around, found the big forum hubs, and lurked away. For months, I read dozens of posts a week, trying to work this world out for myself before saying as much as "boo"—or, "Hi, my name is Pamela and I love dollies." I saw other newbies come up and start posting

Dal Cinnamoroll doll, China, 2008, ©Jun Planning

Hello, Cutie!

everywhere and about everything, and it wasn't long before they were regulars on the "scene," talking casually with the poobahs and answering other people's questions.

Forums are like a club, and within the club there are cliques. On the surface, everybody is very nice and helpful, but inevitably, something is said and misconstrued. Someone gets offended and everyone takes sides. It's really not much different from the "real world" as far as I can tell.

Slowly, I started making a few posts, asking questions, and hoping not to sound too dumb. People were helpful and friendly. I felt relieved if not a bit silly—there was nothing to be afraid of after all. I even found a couple of locals online who collect the same big-eyed gals as I do, and now we meet to take pictures, talk dolls, and chatter about everything else.

Once a cute hunter zeros in on a particular passion, there are all kinds of forums, chat rooms, Etsy teams, Flickr groups, and blogs in which to congregate. Communication is an integral part of cute culture, perhaps now more than ever. With so much doom and gloom in the news, having a community to turn to—in the flesh or online—has become paramount. It's great to have an outlet to post pictures of your cute doll dressed to the nines for an imaginary night on the town. It's also great to have a place to discuss your personal issues, to air frustrations with your work, or seek

support for your health problems. That you only have to hit up a single forum to do all of that is a testament to how close these online communities become.

I think I've seen pretty much every kind of post or topic under the sun on the Blythe doll forum I frequent, but suspect that the two women I've met in person (thanks to the forum) have seen more. I'm curious about their experiences as part of the Blythe community both online and off, so I get in touch with them to get their take on the community aspect of cute culture.

Both Kimberly and Naomi work nine-to-five jobs, so we arrange to meet in a park downtown on a Thursday after they've clocked out. Never one to pass up an opportunity for a mini doll-meet, my daughter tags along, eager to show off her new doll with seafoam-green hair. I pack only one doll—that's all that would fit in my handbag that day—but Naomi turns up with three, and Kimberly four. We line our "girls" up on a bench and snap a few photos before settling in to chat.

When I originally exchanged messages with Kimberly I had no idea that she worked for the newspaper I used to write for. Our time there did overlap, but she worked on the advertising side and I was a writer and editor who worked mostly from home, so our paths hadn't crossed. When we did learn that we'd sort-of worked together, it was one of those delightful

Kimberly Cook (left), Naomi Owen (right), and a few of their Blythe dolls, 2012

feel like I'm such a freak anymore. There's somebody else like me—this is awesome!"

It is awesome to meet up with other connoisseurs and collectors of cute. Kimberly and Naomi both attended the annual BlytheCon in Portland, Oregon, in August 2011 and regale me with stories of their good times. I hear about the dolls, their clothes, and the vendors, but mostly I hear about the people they met and the fun they had. Whether in person or online, it's the people you meet that propel a pastime to a lifestyle and gel a disparate group of people into a full-fledged community, complete with know-it-alls and rabble-rousers. As Kimberly says, sometimes the community contributes to your enjoyment of the hobby in a positive way, but sometimes the impact can be negative. A single comment taken the wrong way, or a straight-up insult, can trigger all sorts of shenanigans. Kimberly, Naomi, and I agree it's best just to stay out of the way in such situations—keep your head down and don't react, and definitely don't post.

No community is without its issues, and those devoted to cute collecting are no exception. I've read some outrageous things in forums; the worst posts are from those who have cast themselves as Judge-of-All-Things. They have an opinion about everything and everyone and don't hesitate to chime in with haughty attitude every time someone makes what they believe is a poor purchase or is

moments: we had even more in common than we'd originally thought.

Kimberly had also met Naomi through the Blythe community online and introduced us. My daughter and I grew the local number of collectors (that we knew of) to four. Sure, that's not even a handful of people, but knowing that just one other person shares your particular passion can bring another dimension to an already enjoyable hobby, by adding both excitement and comfort to the mix. I think Naomi says it best: "It's nice to know that there's another insane person in Calgary that actually shares my crazy love of dolls. I don't

Lineup of Blythe dolls at a local meet in Calgary, 2012. Photo: Emma Klaffke

having a tough time with their boss or family. It's all a bit like being a member of a high-school club—everyone joins because of a shared interest, but there are always going to be one or two troublemakers who can't get past their own biases. Cute culture can get catty, but for the most part the forums and message boards are a great way to meet like-minded people.

Along with the resurgence of handmade, the benefits of community and congregation are certainly key ingredients in the make-up of the new cute, but there's one more element that's too big to ignore. Just as the public

flocked to the movies during the Great Depression, people today have a penchant for escapism, and in the last decade much of that escapism has involved cute. In 2006, cute culture went mega-mainstream with the onset of cute-animal fever.

The psychology of cute (which we'll discuss a bit later in depth) dictates that humans are programmed to interpret big, doleful eyes and soft, round features as cute. The more ridiculous, helpless, and potentially dangerous a situation the cute little kitten or tiny puppy finds itself in, the more likely that "awww" is practically a reflex response. We can't help

Pokémon Squirtle plush, China, 1998, ©Nintendo

Hello, Cutie!

ourselves, it seems. Maternal or paternal feelings—no matter how deeply buried and shunned—are set on full alert. We see baby animals as the cutest little things; they're so clumsy, and we want to help them because they are so ridiculously cute. So we watch and we smile and eventually that "awww" will come, even if we don't say it out loud.

It may sound silly and simplistic, but taking a few minutes out of a busy day to watch a video of a mother cat hugging her kitten makes perfect sense to a lot of us. At heart, I like to think we're pretty silly and simplistic creatures ourselves, and wanting to see cute animals doing cute—albeit sometimes perilous—things is natural. Any short escape we can take from the "real world" is welcome and goes a long way to explaining the seemingly inexplicable and ongoing cute animal phenomenon.

It would be easy to dismiss the cute-animal craze as a fad, like ironic, hipster mustaches or the infamous Pet Rock. But the trend has endured and continues long after what under different circumstances would have surely reached its expiry date several years back. But the desire for photos and YouTube videos featuring cute, hapless creatures shows little sign of waning.

At the core of cute-animal mania is *cuteoverload.com*, a website founded and administered by Meg Frost. The first site to grab worldwide attention by posting photographs of cute animals, it has spawned countless imitators, but remains the go-to spot for your daily fix of cute. Online since 2005, Cute Overload is no longer simply a collection of cute-animal pictures. Now, there are several forms of Cute Overload calendars for sale, including a page-a-day style that can have you saying "awww" all day, every day. Since Cute Overload's Meg Frost is responsible for bringing the cute into so many people's lives, I thought it was time to get her thoughts on the craze she helped create and the reasons for its lasting appeal.

As is the case with so many popular blogs, Cute Overload's success was far from planned. Meg had been curious about blogging and started playing around with software, but she needed content—something just to upload and fill in the blanks as she learned. She'd been collecting photographs of cute animals from around the Internet for some time and chose to use them as her blog content as a matter of convenience more than anything. "I was collecting pictures instead of having an actual pet," she laughs, adding that not only are she and her husband allergic to cats, their room-mate at the time had an allergy to dogs, making pet owning unrealistic. At first, she kept the blog private, but it wasn't long after it went live on September 25, 2005, that Cute Overload became a bona fide sensation. On December 17 of that year, *boingboing.net* published a short

Mystery Rose Tokissi doll, Korea, 2011, ©Tokissi Doll

Hello, Cutie!

item about Cute Overload. The rest, as they say, is history.

"I will never forget that day—hitting refresh [on the site meter] and seeing the numbers," says Meg, who's kindly taking her lunch hour break at her product design day job in the Silicon Valley to speak with me. She quickly realized that Cute Overload had the makings of a brand, and set out to make the name synonymous with the ultimate in cute—or, more aptly, cute with a bite.

What separates Cute Overload from the other cute animal blogs is the writing. The juxtaposition of cute animal photos with snarky cut-lines results in wide appeal and a decidedly modern take on cute. "It's an unusual combination, and I think that's what people like about it," Meg says. She's personally not a fan of the cloying cute, girly world inhabited by the likes of Holly Hobbie and Hello Kitty, and it's that snarky edge that she believes makes Cute Overload appealing to both women and men.

The images may make you squeal with happiness, but it's the text that will make you laugh—no matter who you are or where you're from. "It's so accessible, and not just because of the Internet," says Meg. "Every age likes cute, every culture likes cute—it's this great equalizer." It's also the perfect place to escape on a dark and gloomy day. Meg frequently gets messages from readers who credit Cute Overload with helping them through tough personal issues. It's one site that's guaranteed to perk you up—a "digital anti-depressant," as Meg calls it.

It also serves as a welcome oasis from those relentlessly negative celebrity-bashing gossip blogs. I know I'd rather look at a picture of a tiny kitten or pup yawning adorably than see another photograph of an actress in an unflattering dress or a slideshow featuring stars without makeup. Cute Overload may bring a touch of snark to cute culture, but it's never mean or negative. As Meg Frost so succinctly puts it, "It's not *schadenfreude*, it's a cute kitten."

Those feelings of protectiveness, empathy, and even pity that Cute Overload's endless stream of animal photos stirs in us isn't lost on marketing and advertising executives—or on toy developers. Just as we fawn over actual cute animals, we're prone to do the same when presented with inanimate cute, animal or otherwise. Sure, the new cute promotes a DIY attitude and aesthetic, it brings us together—however unconventionally—and it provides an excellent outlet for escape into a world of rainbows and unicorns, but it also leaves consumers more open than ever to the lures of corporate cute.

The corporatization of cute is not new, but take a stroll through a toyshop and you're sure to notice that the cute dial has been turned up in recent years, with marketers cleverly

Lalaloopsy Featherbed, China, 2010, ©MGA Entertainment

Hello, Cutie!

incorporating elements of community and escapism with social websites and ads featuring elaborate character stories. Look closer, and you'll see how they've widened the eyes of children's favorites such as Strawberry Shortcake and the Care Bears, giving them a more vulnerable—and cute—look. Toy makers know how to play to our sensitivities and tug on our heartstrings: bigger eyes and rounder features will make shoppers weak in the knees, and they won't be able to resist taking the toys home.

Just look at the biggest success story in corporate cuteland in the last few years: Lalaloopsy dolls. Released in late 2010 by MGA Entertainment (the same company responsible for Bratz and Moxie Girlz dolls), the dolls were originally called Bitty Buttons, but that was quickly scrapped in favor of the catchier moniker, Lalaloopsy. I remember seeing news reports and reading about the dolls during the 2010 holiday shopping season. People were mad for them, lining up outside Walmarts and Toys "R" Us stores across North America in hopes of getting their hands on one. Others paid steep prices online, and the dolls sold out.

I'm a sucker for cute, I'm the first to admit. With their black button eyes, colorful hair, and happy smiles, Lalaloopsies are definitely cute, but there was something about them that didn't sit right with me. Perhaps they were too cute? But I think the fact that the press material referred to the dolls with the oversize, hard plastic heads as "rag dolls" bugged me more.

Lalaloopsy is corporate cute at its best (or worst, depending on your point of view). Riffing on the DIY look, the dolls' trademarked tag line is "Sew Magical! Sew Cute!" and according to an official September 2010 press release, the dolls are "a unique and whimsical collection of eight different thirteen-inch (thirty-three-cm) rag dolls who magically came to life when their very last stitch was sewn." Rather than setting off my cute radar, reading this kicked my cynical side into high gear: it's really hard to sew plastic.

Lalaloopsy dolls are still insanely popular and, amusingly enough, soft-bodied rag dolls have been introduced to the line. I still don't get it—I can't buy in, but it's time to see what the fuss is all about, up close. Plus, I know that a local toy liquidation store has them in stock for at least ten dollars less than what they go for elsewhere.

On my way to the store I think about what made these dolls the poster girls for corporate cute. One thing that sets them apart from many previous cute crazes (like Cabbage Patch Kids in the 1980s or Tickle Me Elmo in the '90s) is that it's not just moms buying them for their kids these days. From the outset, adult collectors—mostly women—were hooked on the sweet-looking dolls with cutesy names like Crumbs Sugar Cookie and Blossom Flowerpot.

But, really: sweet or sinister? I was about to find out.

I feel kind of dirty shelling out my $19.99 for one called Pillow Featherbed whose main attribute is that she "loves to sleep." She was also one of the first full-size dolls released. I get her home and hope I can get her out of her elaborate plastic packaging before my daughter gets home from school. Emma doesn't like Lalaloopsies and thinks people should buy handmade rag dolls on Etsy instead.

Pillow Featherbed is cute enough, and I do find myself feeling a bit bad for her, being saddled with all of this corporate cute business. It's completely irrational, but I do think for a moment, *it's not the doll's fault*. I shake this out of my head the best I can, sit her on my desk, and start trolling around Lalaloopsy fan clubs and forums. I see photos on Flickr of fully grown women posing with their collections, and of Lalaloopsy meets. It's not much different than the world of big-eyed Blythe dolls that I inhabit. And they all look so happy, and I can hardly begrudge them that. The new cute—corporate or otherwise—is a bright spot that pops from the bleak. It's a catalyst for connection and a spark for the creative. Everyone is welcome, even Pillow Featherbed.

Look, Mom— I Made It Myself!

FAYTHE LEVINE'S HANDMADE NATION DOCUMENTS AND INSPIRES

Faythe Levine

Photo: Tia Brindel of Little Giant Photography

It's impossible to talk about modern cute culture without discussing how the DIY and handmade movement has influenced it. We all know about online marketplaces like *etsy.com* and its main competitors *artfire.com* and *dawanda.com*, but what's brought it to the fore in recent years? One of the best people to speak to about the handmade movement has to be Faythe Levine, who co-authored (with Cortney Heimerl) the book, *Handmade Nation: The Rise of DIY, Art, Craft, and Design* in 2008, and directed the documentary film of the same name.

Faythe, who runs the Sky High Gallery in Milwaukee in addition to maintaining her own art practice, first caught wind of a show in Chicago called Renegade Craft Fair in 2003. She was accepted as a vendor, and it was this experience that inspired her to start a similar show in Milwaukee, *Art vs. Craft*. She also began forging relationships through online craft forums. "I realized that the momentum of this DIY craft community was strong and thought about capturing that energy," Faythe recalls. "I already knew the importance of cataloging history from a grassroots perspective and was very motivated by the energy around me."

That energy was channeled into the *Handmade Nation* book and film, which became immediate must-haves for both do-it-yourselfers and the culturally curious. "The project reached a much larger audience than I ever expected," says Faythe. "The most common feedback I receive, which makes me feel like it has been successful, is that people feel

Jenine Bressner in her Providence RI studio, 2009; *Handmade Nation* production still. Photo: Faythe Levine

motivated and inspired after watching the movie; it's so awesome to have made something that makes people want to do something."

Four years after the book's release, the handmade community has seen all sorts of shifts and changes. There's no question that it's grown, but with that growth has come obstacles that many crafters didn't foresee, including the practice of major retailers co-opting original designs and products from independent sellers. Faythe has a pragmatic take on this often prickly subject.

"Mainstream retailers will always lift the soul out of small and independent designers. This is partially because the creatives at the mega-agencies are often independent designers by night and work developing products as their day job. The downside of the Internet is the politics of lifting too much inspiration from someone else's work or blatantly reproducing someone's design. However, I think that by having a handmade aesthetic in a mainstream marketplace it makes the 'real' handmade and independently produced work more approachable to a larger market. The catch is that when the general public doesn't understand that if something mass-produced in China looks similar to something that was created in small batches, there is most likely going to be a large price difference. I think the importance of educating the public about production, materials, and labor should be at the forefront of the handmade movement."

The challenges facing the handmade community today are different from those a decade ago, just as the challenges ten years from now will be different still. What's most encouraging is the steady growth and buoyancy of the community, two factors that will be key contributors to the handmade movement that solidify its place in pop culture, rather than simply being a trend or cultural-history aside. Plus, as Faythe Levine reminds us, "People have always made things and sold them and there will always be people who appreciate and buy handmade."

faythelevine.com
skyhighmilwaukee.com
signpaintermovie.com
handmadenationmovie.com
artvscraftmke.com
Twitter: @faythelevine

Hello, Cutie!

My, What Big Eyes You Have

WHEN IT COMES TO CUTE, BIGGER REALLY IS BETTER

I am always being watched. Not by a creepy neighbor, a peeping Tom, or even my fiancé. My daughter and her friends are not spying on me (though they have been known to in the past), but as I sit typing at the desk in my living room, there is no doubt that many eyes are on me.

No, I'm not paranoid, I just have a lot of stuff—cute stuff. A red, anthropomorphic toy piano with a happy face peeks over the top of my computer while beside it, a small ceramic owl stares at something above my head. Six Japanese pose dolls keep a close eye on me from the top of my printer, and one of the Blythe dolls from my collection has migrated from the bedroom to sit perched atop my notes. To the left, there is a spry little elf doll hanging from a hook by the window only inches from an original Lee painting (the artist was known only by that name) of a demure girl clutching a pretty bouquet. To my right, there's a flocked toy lamb, a framed Margaret Keane print, and The Creature, my oldest and most treasured toy.

I think The Creature is supposed to be a bear—a pale yellow bear. He's made of squishy plastic and used to squeak, but now just expels air from the bottom of his left foot when you press his tummy. He stands seven inches tall and is marked "Korea." I have had The Creature since I was a baby. He was a gift, though my mother can't recall from whom, and he's been with me for more than forty years.

The Creature has a big round head, expressive eyes, and a chubby stomach, cute traits he shares with the other objects staring back at me. "Cute" is a hard word to define, when I really stop to think about it. In all of my years of collecting, I've never once looked it up in a dictionary or thought much about what cute

The Creature, vinyl squeak toy, Korea, 1970s, ©Ninohira

Hello, Cutie!

really is. It's one of those things: I know it when I see it. It's an instant reaction. Whether I'm rooting around in a small-town thrift shop or trolling online, when I come across something cute, I instantly want to give it a home.

But what is cute, really? I pull out my giant *Canadian Oxford Dictionary* and look it up. It's a short entry and defines the word as: "1. a. attractive. B. quaintly or affectedly attractive. C. endearing, charming. 2. clever, ingenious, shrewd." It's noted that cute is the shortening of "acute," which may have had some bearing on the word's original use, but is rarely, if ever, used as such today. I cannot imagine anyone thinking The Creature is clever, ingenious, or shrewd when I describe him as cute. But then again, the words attractive, endearing, and charming don't seem to fit either, and I'm left believing that—colloquially, at least—cute is simply cute, no other definition necessary.

What we think is cute and why is an entirely different story, as I soon find out when I start poking around in books and journals. I learn that my attachment to The Creature is perfectly understandable, even normal, and that there is a set of specific aesthetic traits that define "cute."

Imagine this scenario: two mid-century plush kittens sit side-by-side in the display window of a vintage shop. They are both pink and cuddly and they're the same size. But their faces—they're different. You'd take them both, but you can only afford one, so how do you choose? According to the science of cute, chances are you'll pick the one with the biggest eyes, the biggest head, the one that looks the most helpless—even pathetic—to take home. *It needs me*, you think, and the decision is made.

Scientists, savvy marketing executives, and of course, toy designers have long understood that most people naturally respond to neotenous features, which in lay-speak means features like those of babies and children, such as big eyes, small noses and chins, and disproportionately large heads. Women especially are programmed to nurture and protect the smallest and most helpless creatures, and this often extends beyond human-to-human interaction into the realm of human-to-object connection. It turns out I'm not the only one who responds innately to those striking big eyes and turns to mush at the sight of infantile clumsiness, whether it's Winnie the Pooh getting his snout stuck in a honey jar or an actual toddler taking her first awkward steps.

The weird science of cute has been well documented by psychologists and anthropologists, but it's the work of the late Austrian scientist Konrad Lorenz that's most notable. A Nobel Prize-winning ethologist, ornithologist, and zoologist, Lorenz asserted that humans are equipped with aesthetic evaluation feelings. In other words, I got this one right:

Trio of vinyl Kewpie dolls, 1970s

Hello, Cutie!

we know cute when we see it. And big eyes and big heads are intrinsically linked to our concept of cute. Throughout the twentieth century and into the twenty-first, many of the most popular dolls and playthings found on toy-store shelves have possessed these features. One of the earliest cuties was the Kewpie doll, inspired by American illustrator Rose O'Neill's successful drawings in *Ladies' Home Journal* magazine. Dolls were introduced to the American market as German-made ceramic bisque dolls in 1913, and later as celluloid and then vinyl versions. Prior to Kewpie, most dolls and toys had been designed to resemble the real-life forms they were modeled after. So, for the most part, baby dolls looked like babies, and teddy bears were crafted to look like bears. The Kewpie, however, doesn't look one bit like any baby I've ever seen with its naked, cherubic shape, curlicue tuft of hair, and big, googly eyes.

The Kewpie was the first full-fledged cute craze, with some sources putting sales of Kewpie dolls and merchandise at over five million pieces in the 1910s. It's also been a craze that's endured. A century later, Kewpies are still being licensed, produced, and sold. Collectors covet early Kewpies—many of which were given as carnival prizes—and these can fetch upwards of $1,000 each.

There are countless Kewpies out there. I log onto eBay and find over 1,600 listings, ranging from children's books to a Kewpie-shaped light bulb, figurines promoting 7-Eleven stores in Hong Kong and, of course, the classic dolls. I also discover that Kewpie madness runs much deeper than I had originally thought. There's an organization called the International Rose O'Neill Club Foundation, and their showcase event is the annual Kewpie celebration, Kewpiesta, that's been held in Branson, Missouri, near Rose O'Neill's hometown of Bonniebrook, since 1968.

I need to know more about Kewpies and the Kewpie people, so I track down Susan Wilson, the president of the International Rose O'Neill Club Foundation. A retired first-grade teacher, Susan has been a Kewpie fan since she first attended the Rose O'Neill Week celebrations in Branson in 1967. A long-time doll collector, Susan was smitten by the cute Kewpie and soon drawn into its creator's fascinating life story.

"Rose was an amazing woman—she had a natural talent for drawing, poetry, storytelling and [a strong] interest in women's rights. Her creative genius was used to provide for her family, friends, and others," says Susan, who not only collects Kewpies, but all things Rose O'Neill, including books and original art.

Rose O'Neill's business smarts are almost as legendary as her talents. She locked down all rights to her Kewpie dolls and was known as a shrewd negotiator and pioneer of licensing

Pose doll heads, Japan, 1960s

Hello, Cutie!

deals. It's all pretty impressive stuff, especially considering that American women didn't win the right to vote nationwide until 1920.

Kewpies, however, were more than a business venture for Rose O'Neill. As Susan Wilson explains, the dolls and their stories—which captured the imaginations of both children and adults of the time—were an outlet for O'Neill to share a philosophy of acceptance, kindness, and tolerance regardless of age or nationality. The Kewpie, as Susan says, is an icon of happiness the world over, a legacy that continues to this day. I challenge any cute hunter to resist the charms of the doll that Susan Wilson describes so rightly as "a chubby little elf-like creature with a top knot of hair, laughing eyes and sweet smile."

Even though the original Kewpies were made from hard materials like bisque, their clever design makes them infinitely cuddly. Since I'm from the plastics age, I have only known Kewpies as molded, rubbery dolls. I have three in my collection, identical and nicknamed The Triplets. They're marked Hong Kong, and I bought them in the mid-1990s at the infamous Toronto discount store Honest Ed's. There was a bin full of them, and they were a dollar or two each—a major bargain by today's escalating prices for vintage dolls produced in certain Asian countries.

Dolls and toys made in Japan, Korea, Hong Kong, and Taiwan—before production of just

A rare kewpie belonging to Mrs. Carey Brown of Shorewood, Illinois. Photo: © Flash Photo

about everything moved to China—are increasingly sought-after, as has been the case with pose dolls, which are display dolls rather than ones designed for play. Three years ago, I couldn't have told you what a pose doll was, but once photos started turning up on online photography sites like Flickr, the more I had to have one.

The most familiar pose doll is the Southern Belle type, with big, Scarlet O'Hara dresses and fanciful hairdos. Made of flesh-colored stockinette, Styrofoam, and wire, they were the dolls that people's grandmothers had

Blythe All Gold in One "Goldie" doll, China, 2001, ©Hasbro/CWC/Takara

Hello, Cutie!

displayed on living room side tables with a crocheted doily underneath. They were inexpensive and considered tasteless by many, and heaps of them ended up in rummage sales and thrift shops. Now those "tasteless" dolls are chased down by collectors from around the world, and it's rare to find a cheap one second-hand.

With their hand-painted faces and flexible limbs, pose dolls were manufactured primarily in Japan and Korea, with loads of them ready for export to the West. Companies like Holiday Fair, Herman Pecker, Voguemont, and the biggest—Bradley—churned dolls out at a rapid pace throughout the 1960s and '70s. There were the tall, mini-skirted Herman Pecker mod girls, the fairy-tale inspired Holiday Fair dolls, Voguemont's well-dressed girly ladies, and too many kinds of Bradleys to count. Crafty types could also make their own versions of pose dolls by purchasing ready-made heads and instruction booklets at hobby shops, creating their bodies with plastic bottles or dressing them in wide, hand-knit skirts that doubled as toilet paper cozies.

I have an even dozen scattered around my home, from tall, lanky Herman Pecker mod "Jody" twins to Little Miss Muffet and Little Red Riding Hood to one that's inexplicably dressed in a pink velveteen elephant costume. For static dolls that aren't played with, they have a surprising amount of individuality, some of which comes from their costumes, but most of which is expressed in their big, lively eyes.

Not everyone wants a doll that's just for display. Lots of us want something we can play with, a doll we can dress up without worrying too much if she face-plants onto the grass while we're playing outside. Play value is undoubtedly one of the factors that has made Blythe the undisputed queen of the big-eyed dolls.

She's also one of the most divisive. Some people think she's the cutest doll, while others find her odd and a little bit scary. Me? I've experienced life on both sides of the Blythe divide. I leafed through the book *This Is Blythe* by Gina Garan when it was published in 2000, but I didn't encounter Blythe in person until I saw her in 2003 at the Kidrobot store in New York City. The shop was carrying the newly released Petite Blythes as well as the boxy Blythe Kubrick figurines. I snapped up a few of both, and when I got home considered buying a full-size Neo Blythe online, but was too busy working and caring for a toddler to pursue it. But I never completely forgot about Blythe. Working as a pop-culture columnist, I came across her name every once in a while, and I got my hands on a copy of Garan's *Blythe Style* book when it was published in 2005. A year later, Blythe officially became part of my life when a friend bequeathed a vintage Blythe to me and my daughter.

Blow mold display head, 1960s

Hello, Cutie!

In the doll world, the story of Blythe is legendary and unique. She was first introduced to North American kids by Kenner in 1972, but was hardly a success. Her big eyes, which change color with a pull-string placed in the back of her head, and giant head are said to have terrified children, and the line was dropped after only one year. She was handed a second life in 2000, when Gina Garan's book was published. It was a hit, and a year later Blythe was starring in Japanese television ads and modeling for the American department store Nordstrom. The Japanese company Cross World Communications (CWC) introduced the first Neo Blythe, a reproduction of the failed '70s doll, that same year.

The original vintage dolls—known in the Blythe community simply as "Kenners"—saw their prices skyrocket, and by the mid-2000s, were selling for $800–$1,000 USD (or more) each. That we had a Kenner in the house would have been a big deal for many collectors, but like many of the kids who had been given Blythes more than thirty years before, my daughter was terrified of the thing and banished it from her bedroom, and then from mine.

It was nonsensical, I know, but I felt bad for the doll, having to hide it behind some books on a shelf too high for my daughter to accidentally stumble upon. So we talked about it and then we gave it away.

Another five years passed. It wasn't until we discovered another big-eyed doll called Dal that we were led back to Blythe. My daughter and I both liked Dals and quickly collected a few, the first of which came from Gina Garan, ironically enough. We started sewing Dal clothes, and I read somewhere that they would likely also fit Blythe. I found a second-hand one online, but wasn't expecting to respond to it so enthusiastically. After all, we'd had a Blythe in the house before.

I adored my Blythe doll and named her Mackenzie, but my daughter wasn't so sure. At first, she thought it was "creepy," but after spending some time playing with Mackenzie, she warmed to her and soon had two dolls of her own, Janie and Jasmine. We made them clothes and styled their hair. We wrapped Christmas presents for them and placed them under the tiny doll-sized tree in her bedroom.

This is completely normal, at least among Blythe collectors, who are some of the most devoted doll aficionados around. Forget Barbie. Compared to Blythe, she's dull and expressionless. They may be the same height, but Blythe is the one with the big personality, and the emotional attachment that owners have with their dolls may have a lot to do with the science of cute. Her big eyes and oversized head are two of the key traits scientists have identified as emotional triggers that help define cute. We want to look after our Blythe

From *Susie Says* by Gina Garan and Justin Vivian Bond, published by powerHouse Books

dolls and take good care of them. Among collectors Blythe is never referred to as an "it," but a "she" or "her." There is much discussion about what to do if you don't "bond" with your girl, and you would never sell a doll, but instead "re-home" her or put her up for adoption. Thousands of collectors can spend hundreds of dollars for just one outfit by a well-known Blythe designer (yes, there are well-known Blythe designers), and forking over several hundred dollars for customized faces and re-rooted hair is also common.

The human characteristics Blythe lovers assign to their dolls may seem strange to some—especially considering many collectors are professionals in their thirties and forties—but for many collectors, the dolls serve as a much-needed creative outlet in their lives. You can develop a doll's personality to your taste, give her a back-story, make her clothes, photograph her, build her a house—there are endless possibilities.

Few dolls inspire the way Blythe does, but one vintage big-eyed girl is fast gaining popularity: Susie Sad Eyes. Introduced in the mid-'60s, Susie Sad Eyes is a small doll, standing eight inches (twenty cm) high, with enormous eyes. She is either a blonde or a brunette and

Hello, Cutie!

"The Internet connection was so slow last night I had to use my imagination."

From *Susie Says* by Gina Garan and Justin Vivian Bond, published by powerHouse Books

has especially pale skin, which gives her sort of a gothic look. She wears demure dresses and tights, and has two friends, Susie Slicker (who wears a plastic raincoat) and Soul Sister, her African-American pal. Her expression is static—her eyes don't move or close. To me, she always looks disappointed, like her parents have just told her they're canceling the family vacation.

Susie was one of a peculiar wave of dolls that included Lonely Lisa and Love Me Linda, girls with a hopeful look in their big eyes that must have screamed from the toy-store shelves, "Pick me! Pick me!" It's not hard to imagine mothers shopping for gifts for their daughters and being sucked into a vortex of sympathy for these despondent creatures. What would be the reaction of those daughters? Imagine that it's her birthday or Christmas, an occasion she's been anticipating for weeks, maybe months. She's expecting a doll, hoping for a Barbie or Tressy or a stylish mod Alta Moda Furga girl. She tears open the gift wrap and there she is: Lonely Lisa, Love Me Linda, Susie Sad Eyes, or one of her friends. The only thing I can picture the girl doing is bursting into tears.

Dolls play a very different role in a child's

"The only thing I can really trust
is my own self-indulgence."

From *Susie Says* by Gina Garan and Justin Vivian Bond, published by powerHouse Books

life than an adult's. While Mom may not have been able to resist bringing a sad doll home, kids generally want glamorous, aspirational dolls or ones that mirror her own age and general appearance. No little girl I know wants a sad-looking doll, and when I show my daughter Susie Sad Eyes, she wants nothing to do with her. Her sympathy button has been pushed too hard; the doll, she says, is too sad.

Perhaps Susie, *et al.*, should be left to the grownups. Interest in these "pre-Blythe" dolls, as they are often referred to, is growing, and in spring 2012, Blythe's fairy godmother, Gina Garan, saw a new book of photographs pub-

lished, this time featuring Susie Sad Eyes. A collaboration with New York performer Justin Vivian Bond, *Susie Says* will surely draw greater attention to Miss Sad Eyes. Twelve years after the publication of *This Is Blythe*, what made Gina switch her focus, and what is it exactly about Susie Sad Eyes that captured her imagination?

Sitting here thinking of such questions won't get me anywhere, so I send a message to Gina to see if she has time for a little Susie Sad Eyes chat. A lifelong fan of dolls from the 1960s and '70s, Gina always had a soft spot for Susie and her big-eyed gal pals. She still loves

Hello, Cutie!

"In
the
end
it
will
be
the
eccentric
people
who
will
make
the
world
worth
saving."

From *Susie Says* by Gina Garan and Justin Vivian Bond, published by powerHouse Books

Blythe, but Susie has that certain *je ne sais quoi* that inspired Gina to delve right into another dolly adventure. "Susie seems quieter than Blythe," Gina explains, "It's like she's thinking—there's something behind her eyes."

It's easy to see how Susie's pensive expression can be interpreted as a subdued thoughtfulness; she's a dark teenaged girl, always thinking, but too shy to say too much. After talking with Gina about Susie and reading the quippy thoughts that accompany Gina's photographs in *Susie Says*, I start to see Susie in a new light. She reminds me a little of my own junior high-school self: simultaneously sullen and hopeful, smart-alecky and insecure. I understand why Gina plucked Susie from her collection of more than 3,000 dolls and gave her a new life.

I'm also excited to learn that Susie's new life doesn't stop with the book. Gina has partnered with an Asian toy company, and a revamped Susie Sad Eyes doll will hit the market in 2013. The dolls will have the same Susie head and face we have come to know, but her body—which, like most of the dolls of her era, was stubby with limited movement—will be completely articulated with bending joints. With Gina's touch, the new Susie will likely

Ceramic mouse, Japan, 1960s

Hello, Cutie!

be the next dolly star. I can see it now: collectors clamoring for original dolls will drive up online auction prices in the process; a cottage industry of Susie-specific doll fashion designers will be spawned; and photographers who use the sad-eyed girl as their muse will flood the pages of image-sharing sites like Flickr.

The new Susie will also undoubtedly coax dollars from the pocketbooks of those of us suffering from a chronic case of "dolly empathy." I laugh with Gina about this affliction that we share. "Sometimes I'll see a doll in a store window that's not in great shape, but I feel that I have to rescue it," she says. I know exactly what she's talking about. It's hard to ignore that beaten-up dolly at the bottom of the thrift store bin. If it has big sad eyes, it's even harder. Members of the dolly empathy league can see the potential in hard-luck cases: all they need is a wash, a makeover, and a little care.

The dolly empathy situation is bad enough with second-hand dolls, but the thought of toy-store shelves with stacks of sad dolls is almost too much to bear. Susie Sad Eyes with her melancholy stare is one thing, but she has nothing on the saddest sad-sack doll of the 1960s.

That would be Little Miss No Name, who was released by Hasbro in 1965 but didn't last long. The nameless big-eyed doll resembles a street urchin. She's barefoot and clothed in a patched-up burlap dress. She appears to be begging and has a giant tear falling from one eye. I am very liberal in my dolly tastes, and even if something isn't for me, I can usually see how others may find it appealing. But Little Miss No Name makes me feel like my daughter did upon first seeing Susie Sad Eyes: she's just too sad. The only thing worse might be finding a doll in its original box, which had this disturbing ditty printed on it: "I need someone to love me. I want to learn to play / Please take me home with you / and brush my tear away."

Today, it's unlikely that any of the big American toy companies would dream of mass-producing a sad doll. The closest they've come in recent years has been Mattel's American Girl doll line, which in 2009 released "Gwen Thompson," a homeless girl who lives in a car with her mom. But a "homeless" doll that retails for close to $100 seems more tacky and exploitive than sad.

I can't look at Little Miss No Name for very long, and Gwen Thompson strikes me as a giant marketing misstep, so I move on to the pathetic but infinitely more comical Pity Kitties. Maybe it's their cartoonish look, but it's hard for me to take the Pity Kitties—or their doggie counterparts, the Pity Puppies—seriously.

A part of the 1960s sad-eyes phenomenon, Pity Kitties and Puppies were the subjects of a vast number of paintings and prints by an artist known only as Gig, whose success inspired

Char-Lee Original, oil on wood, USA, 1960s, ©Lee

Hello, Cutie!

imitators and prompted the manufacture of various wares featuring the pathetic, giant-eyed animals. Ceramic figurines and piggy banks were common, but it was the artwork that was—and still is—most in demand.

Gig was one of several painters who adopted the style of painting big-eyed portraits in the 1960s, including artists known as Eden, Maio, Lee, Goji, and more. By far the most famous of the big-eye artists is Margaret Keane, though it was her then-husband, Walter, whose name the paintings originally appeared under starting in the early 1960s. It wasn't until 1986—years after the Keanes' divorce—when Margaret was able to wrestle out from under her husband's shadow once and for all and claim her much-overdue recognition. Doing so involved a drawn-out federal court case during which Margaret demonstrated her painting skills by creating a portrait in the courtroom (Walter refused the challenge, citing a sore shoulder as an excuse). More than two decades after the first "Keane Eyes" paintings were brought to market, she was fully acknowledged as the artist behind the famous pictures.

Margaret Keane's work has always been an easy target for art critics, who often dismiss it as kitsch and lowbrow. This hasn't sapped the pride of avid Keane collectors, whose ranks have included erstwhile stars like Dean Martin, Jerry Lewis, and Liberace, and contemporary celebrities such as Marilyn Manson,

Tim Burton, and pop star Matthew Sweet. Keane painted commissioned portraits of Joan Crawford and Natalie Wood and still accepts commissions to this day through her Keane Eyes Gallery, which she opened in San Francisco in 1991.

I would love to have a portrait of my daughter done and think I may have to inquire about a commission soon, or at least before the film *Big Eyes* is released, and more people are exposed to Keane's work. After being kicked around Hollywood development hell for years, the long-anticipated bio-pic based on Keane's life is going ahead in 2012, with Tim Burton producing, and Ryan Reynolds and Reese Witherspoon starring as Walter and Margaret.

If I am able to solicit a commission, it's probably best I show my daughter examples of Keane's work post-Walter, after she moved to Hawaii and started using cheery colors and festive backgrounds. Long gone are the lonely waifs in dark alleys, but the eyes are as big as ever and unmistakably Keane's. My one Keane print—titled *Rejected* and dated 1962—sits propped on a skinny yellow vintage Arborite table to the right of my desk. It's partially obscured by a decorative green glass bowl from the '70s and can't been seen if you're sitting on the sofa watching television. My daughter wouldn't have it any other way, as she can't bear to look at the young crying girl portrayed in the print. Like Susie Sad Eyes and

My, What Big Eyes You Have

Li'l Peepers' Jovita hippopotamus plush, China, 2007, ©Russ Berrie

Hello, Cutie!

her gang of similarly forlorn friends, she finds *Rejected* simply *too* sad.

Too sad or not, the emotional connection we establish with Keane's art is undeniable. As the saying goes, it's all in the eyes, something Margaret Keane understands and Osamu Tezuka clearly understood. The Japanese artist responsible for such legendary animated series and films as *Testuwan Atomu*—better known in the West as *Astro Boy*—and *Kimba the White Lion*, Tezuka is widely considered a pop-culture pioneer and the man responsible for establishing the big, rounded head and giant eyes style of anime we still know today. It's said that he believed that oversized eyes best revealed and conveyed emotion, and while Astro Boy may not have had hearts popping from his eyes like so many anime characters today do, his large eyes have almost certainly contributed to his enduring success and influence on the manga and anime industries.

Tezuka honed his signature big-eyes-and-heads style after World War II. His graphic novel, *Shin Takarajima*—or *New Treasure Island*—was published in 1947, sixteen years before his *Astro Boy* anime debuted as Japan's first homegrown animated television series. By this time, other Japanese animators and cartoonists had adopted Tezuka's style and soon the big-head-and-eyes look was branded distinctly Japanese, though it likely was rooted in early American animation. Disney characters such as Mickey Mouse and Donald Duck were created in the 1920s and '30s, and like their later Japanese counterparts had big eyes. Disney characters are believed to have informed Tezuka's work, but not nearly to the extent that his work, namely *Kimba the White Lion*, later informed Disney's. *The Lion King* is regarded as a blatant copy of *Kimba*, an issue so often discussed in animation circles that it became the punch line of a joke on *The Simpsons* in 1995.

Given the choice, I know that my daughter would choose *Kimba* over *The Lion King's* Simba any day. She was bitten by the anime bug at age eight, first by *Pokémon*, and then by quirky series like *Fruits Basket* and *Rozen Maiden*. Her love of anime overlapped with another big-eye obsession: collecting a line of stuffed animals called Li'l Peepers. The original "Peepers" was a small plush mouse by the same name manufactured in the late 1970s. The toy with the glassy, outsized eyes didn't spawn a line of stuffed animals at the time, but nearly three decades later, the American toy company Russ Berrie released Li'l Peepers, much to the delight of my daughter and her friends.

From Kewpies to Peepers, a century of cute has been dominated by creatures with big eyes and heads. The look is readily associated with cute even if we're not conscious of that link when we're watching anime or shelling out for adorable dolls and plush toys whose emotive eyes tell us that we're the ones to give them a home.

Walking Musical Series piano, Japan, 1970s

Hello, Cutie!

Strike a Pose

LADY-LIKE DOLLS HAVE TURNED
COLLECTOR KATIE BARKER
INTO A "DOLLAHOLIC"

Katie Barker

Photo: Elle Mohan

Vintage Japanese pose dolls are the strangest thing. I don't mean they're weird, but it is strange how difficult it is to dish on these elegant dollies' past. Even UK-based collector Katie Barker knows only bits and pieces of their history, and trust me, if anyone would have the skinny on vintage Japanese pose dolls, it would be her.

Katie figures that she first encountered pose dolls as a child thirty years ago, but it wasn't until the late 1990s and early 2000s when online shopping and auction sites really took off that her collection began in earnest. Since then, over 300 dolls have passed through her home in Surrey, England, and in 2006 she set up an Etsy shop in which she deals in vintage pose dolls and greeting cards—her other great collecting passion.

While pose dolls were staples in Japanese homes in the 1960s, it's only been in recent years that avid interest from collectors in the West have driven demand—and prices—up. Katie takes it all in stride, remaining as enthusiastic a collector as ever, always on the hunt for a rare or unusual piece.

"It's almost impossible to say what draws me to a particular pose doll, but when I purchase one I revert back to being an eight-year-old child again. [When] it arrives, it takes pride of place in my house and every other doll suddenly gets shunned into the background. In time, another doll will catch my eye, and I will love her even more. Before you know it, the doll I thought I could never part with is up for sale in my shop. I am like a dollaholic."

For Katie, the unique characteristics of pose dolls set them apart from other toys and novelties of the same era. "The pose doll is a class of doll all of her own," Katie explains. "She is not like any other [doll] of her day, and I don't think we have seen anything similar since. [It's] the attention to detail in each hand-painted face, the fabulous molding of their heads, and their shiny silky wigs."

While hard facts about pose doll history may be scarce, one thing we do know is that the dolls' greatest heyday was in the mod '60s, and for those of us like Katie Barker who weren't around to witness that era first-hand, collecting pose dolls allows us to give in to our vintage fashion fantasies. "These dolls allow us to indulge in the past and enjoy the mini skirt, PVC dresses, hippie bell-bottom trousers, and wonderful striking makeup [of the 1960s]. They represent many types of faces and even ethnicity. They show women to be fun as well as confident, and they do not look out of place in the most modern of homes—they have a uniqueness that makes them talking pieces for their owners," Katie says, before adding, "and every doll has a story to tell."

Etsy: poshtottydesignz.etsy.com
Folksy: folksy.com/shops/poshtottydesignz
Flickr: flickr.com/photos/40731889@
    N08/sets/72157622600035056/

Poi, one in Katie Barker's amazing pose doll collection, sitting in an Art Deco tea cup.
Photo: Katie Barker

Mallory, one in Katie Barker's amazing pose doll collection — a girl with an incredibly rare face.
Photo: Katie Barker

Hello, Cutie!

Big-Eyed Beauty

Fanny Zara

Photo: Roz Boatman

Don't call Fanny Zara's interest in Blythe dolls a hobby. The forty-year-old working mother of two is adamant that her dolls are a passion, not a mere pastime. "Blythe dolls are the first objects I ever collected, and I collect these specific dolls only. I am talking about passion when it comes to Blythe because I feel it is more intense and obsessive than what I call a hobby. That doll conveys a lot of strong and sometimes even extreme emotions."

That intense response to Blythe started for Fanny in 2008, when she came across the doll on the blog, *www.weewonderfuls.com*. It was love at first sight, but for French-born Fanny, who now lives in Canada, there was a lot more to be done before she took the plunge and bought a doll of her own. "It took me six months to buy my first Blythe, as I wanted to know everything about the doll first to help me make up my mind. There were so many and all so different!"

By the time she did finally settle on a doll in the first half of 2009—a limited edition Blythe Amaryllis with bright-green hair—she was hooked and already immersed in Blythe culture. Within the year she had started her blog Mademoiselle Blythe (*blythe-doll-fashions. com*) and was sharing her knowledge and conducting interviews with Blythe customizers and fellow collectors.

As the blog has grown, so has Fanny's devotion to the dolls and the community of collectors that motivates her. "I am fascinated by artists and fashion designers and it is so interesting to get to know them better, find out how they got into Blythe, and understand what inspires them." She says, "Blythe is the best way for me to combine everything I love and want to be part of my life: art, fashion, beauty. I am moved by anything I find beautiful. It can be a work of art, a book, a movie, a song, a jacket, a pair of shoes, a poem or a doll. Blythe moves me and makes me happy just looking at her."

. . . .

Blog: blythe-doll-fashions.com/
Flickr: flickr.com/photos/mademoiselleblythe/
Facebook: facebook.com/fanny.zara
Twitter: @fannyzara

Fanny's dolls at home. Photo: Fanny Zara

Fanny's favourite Blythe doll, Anaïs.
Photo: Fanny Zara

Hello, Cutie!

The Eyes Have It

Megan Besmirched

Photo: Megan Besmirched

Megan Besmirched knows exactly who's responsible for triggering her infatuation with big-eyed art: the folks behind the children's magazine *Humpty Dumpty*. It was the ads for prints of baby animals with over-sized eyes that she first saw in the publication that introduced her to what would become an important interest and influence on her own work as an artist herself.

"I had an affinity for big-eyed art as a little kid. [But it wasn't] until I was a little older that I had the chance to actively seek it out. I started collecting prints from saving my lunch money and going to rummage sales and charity shops, buying prints for a nickel or two. At the time, I had no idea it was some-thing that I would later be influenced by. I just loved the imagery," Megan says.

The California native who now calls Chicago home has an extensive collection of work by renowned big-eyed artists like Keane, Eden, Igor Pantuhoff, and Megan's personal favorite, Gig. She's also a fabulous source of information about the artists and their era. In fact, she's compiled a book, *Big-Eyed Masters*, about the subject. She rattles off artist's names, characterizing their work with ease.

Even in her pre-Internet teenage days, Megan was bent on researching big-eyed art and the artists behind it. In a serendipitous twist, she discovered that Walter Keane lived only ten minutes from her childhood home. She met him shortly after graduating from high school and from there her appetite for learning more about other big-eyed artists grew. She pieced together bits of informa-tion from other collectors and eventually began meeting with the artists' relatives to get to know the details of their professional and personal lives. All the while, her collection grew and her own art practice developed. After so many years surrounded by big-eyed art, it's no wonder that subtle shades of the big-eyed Masters surface in her own portraits of "sweet doll-faced girls with tattoos," as she describes them.

"I think I feed off of the 'vibe' of the style," she says. "I was so consumed with my research that my actual painting evolved from being surrounded by all the hundreds of things that I have collected, seen, and researched. I like the style and the mood, and that is what is inspiring. I don't reference anything when I am working on something...so it comes from within, but it is quite obvious where my sources lie."

. . . .

besmirched.com
saltydame.com
Twitter: @besmirched
Facebook: facebook.com/meganbesmirched
Etsy: etsy.com/shop/besmirched

Megan Besmirched paintings. Acrylic on canvas, 2011.
Top to Bottom:
"Black Heart,"
"Pink Lady,"
"Big Hair Big Heart."
Photos: Megan Besmirched

Megan Besmirched. Acrylic on canvas, 2012. "Sworn To Fun"

Eden. Oil on canvas. "Untitled." From the collection of Megan Besmirched

Hello, Cutie!

Big in Japan

MORE THAN ANY OTHER, ONE NATION DRIVES THE "CUTE ECONOMY"

I was five years old when I fell under the spell of Hello Kitty. Like so many of my schoolmates' fathers, my dad went on frequent business trips to far-flung places, and in 1976 he began making annual visits to Japan in the spring, a routine that would last twenty-five years, all the way up to his retirement. The 1970s and early '80s were the heyday of international business travel. Big companies pulled out all the stops in an effort to impress their guests, treating them to the best food and drink, sometimes even picking up the tab for their spouses to join them, and always making sure they went home with plenty of gifts.

My brother and I used to call them "prizes." As soon as Dad stepped through the door, we'd squirm with impatience until he started to unpack and we could see what loot he'd brought back. The best companies always knew how many children a guest had and

their gender and age, and would be sure to include something for each member of the family. They were often small toys—a figurine, maybe a necklace—all crafted in the traditional style of the country he visited. But of all the countries, the "prizes" from Japan were always the best.

My dad would often pick up extra things for us as well—he'd ask his foreign colleagues and interpreters about the popular kids' stuff, and that's how he was introduced to Hello Kitty. She was still relatively new in Japan, but had gained quick success since her launch two years earlier, in 1974. I think he brought me stickers and a small stationery set—tiny pencils and a pad in a transparent plastic case. One look at the sweet kitty with the red bow and no mouth, and I was sold. Hello Kitty was the cutest thing I had ever seen. I didn't know much about Japan or cute culture or much of anything, really—except that I wanted more.

Ceramic Hello Kitty, China, 2011, ©Sanrio Co., Ltd.

Hello, Cutie!

There's no way my dad could have known how those tiny Hello Kitty items he gave me in 1976 would affect me, but for thirty-five years that sweet cat has been in my life in some form or other. Only a couple of years after our first introduction, I was thrilled to find Hello Kitty merchandise tucked away in small Japanese gift shops in California while vacationing with my family, and by the time I was ten, her face started popping up in local shops as well. Fast forward fifteen years, and the first boyfriend I lived with gave me a Hello Kitty cereal bowl I still have; another friend gave me a clock for my twenty-eighth birthday; and I bought myself a pair of puffy Kitty slippers at the now-defunct Sanrio store in San Francisco the following year. Don't get me wrong: I don't live in a pink palace surrounded by all things Hello Kitty, but the pieces I do have always bring a smile to my face.

There's no astonishing explanation for Hello Kitty's worldwide success. Even the executives at Sanrio, the company that created her, have no sure answers. I dust off my copy of Hello Kitty's corporate biography, *Hello Kitty: The Remarkable Story of Sanrio and the Billion Dollar Feline Phenomenon* by Ken Belson and Brian Bremner, and skim the chapter, "The God of Kawaii," about Sanrio's founder, Shintaro Tsuji. When asked by the authors in 2002 about Hello Kitty's remarkable popularity, his answer was decidedly candid:

"In thirty-five years, Sanrio has made 450 characters. But, of course, really only one was a real hit: Kitty. The longest of the characters lasted for just seven years, but only Kitty lasted longer. I have no idea why Kitty has lasted this long."

Others have speculated about Hello Kitty's appeal, with many concluding that it's her innocence and girlishness that spark cuddly memories of childhood. Some share my theory that she's different from American characters in the sense that she wasn't originally spawned from a film or television show like so many of the toys we had growing up. She didn't come with a built-in personality, and perhaps this made it easy to imagine Kitty any way we wished.

Sanrio did provide Hello Kitty with a short background story, but it was never greatly promoted and only occasionally referred to until the debut of the first Hello Kitty television anime in 1987. I didn't know anything about her "life" until the mid-1990s when I happened upon her fictional history online. In case you didn't know already, Hello Kitty's real name is Kitty White. She's not Japanese but English and lives in suburban London with her family, including her twin sister, Mimmy, who looks identical to Kitty but wears her bow on the opposite ear. Kitty's birthday is November 1 (which I guess makes her a Scorpio). She is five apples tall and weighs three apples,

Big-eyed mouse cabin, Japan, 1960s

Hello, Cutie!

though no standard of "apple weight" or "apple height" is given, so you'll have to use your imagination.

Hello Kitty's simple design likely contributes to the attraction as well, though one of her signature features—or lack thereof—has been a point of contention. Except in the five animated series she's starred in, Hello Kitty famously has no mouth. Some purists were not impressed with a televised, bemouthed Kitty that could speak, while others have complained about her mouthlessness. Certain feminists believe that the fact that Kitty cannot speak supports an antiquated stereotype of female submissiveness.

I find it improbable that many Hello Kitty fans have given much thought to any potentially sinister, anti-women subtext when purchasing a Kitty handbag, Kitty jewelry, even a limited-edition Kitty car or vibrator. The number of products that Hello Kitty's image has appeared on is mind-boggling, as are the countless licensing deals Sanrio has made since Kitty's resurgence in the 1990s.

There has been a Hello Kitty toaster, a Fender Stratocaster guitar, and even Hello Kitty wine. It's said that Sanrio will consider licensing to companies of all sorts, the only no-no being tobacco. But this kind of brand ubiquity can be damaging, resulting in consumer fatigue, something Hello Kitty seems to have been afflicted with since the

Ceramic and fake-fur dog, Japan, 1960s, ©Giftcraft

start of the new century. Sales of Kitty merchandise has been on the decline for more than a decade, and in 2002 Kitty fell from the top spot in a ranking of Japan's most popular characters by Character Databank, a research company that bases its yearly rankings on sales of character goods.

Kitty's profits and popularity may be shrinking, but there is no shortage of new characters angling to take her place. The character goods market in Japan is fiercely competitive, and Sanrio's main rival, San-X, has been gaining ground with characters like Tarepanda and Rilakkuma. And goods featuring new anime

Jody pose doll, Japan, 1960s, ©Herman Pecker & Co., Inc.

Hello, Cutie!

characters continue to grow, just as old favorites like Pokémon and Anpanman enjoy a renaissance.

But if it wasn't for Sanrio's Shintaro Tsuji and Hello Kitty, many of the super-cute items we've come to associate with Japan might not exist. He built his empire around gift giving—among Japanese girls in particular, who are known to bestow upon each other small presents of good will. Naturally, if someone gives you a friendship gift, you should reciprocate by giving her one. She'll, of course, feel obliged to give you another as a thank-you for your gift, and so on—this cycle could continue indefinitely.

Friendship gifts weren't the only market Tsuji had in mind for products. He knew of the tradition of exchanging birthday presents popular in the West and took it upon himself to introduce and encourage this practice in Japan. It's a country where gift-giving was already an ingrained custom, so it's no surprise that the habit of giving birthday presents was quickly embraced. That Shintaro Tsuji started Sanrio in 1960 undoubtedly played a key role in the company's success. His timing couldn't have been better: right smack in the middle of Japan's Showa era.

"Cute Japan" was hatched and evolved during this period, from 1926 to 1989, when the Showa Emperor, Hirohito, reigned. After World War II and the recovery of Japan's

Treasure Pet squirrel, Japan, 1960s

sovereignty in 1952, the country's leaders—with aid from the United States—not only rebuilt the economy in record time, they saw it flourish. By the 1960s, Japan had become a major exporter to the West, and it was during this time that Japanese cute as we know it today started to wash up on our shores. Ceramic figurines, chalkware, and stuffed animals were some of the common items we'd find in local shops marked "Made in Japan," but it's the dolls that have become the most prized treasures for many cute collectors.

Japan's relationship with dolls was hardly new by the time the Showa era rolled around, even though some of the types of dolls may

Wooden kokeshi doll, Japan, 1980s

Hello, Cutie!

have been. One of the oldest types of Japanese doll is the *kokeshi*. Made of smooth, carved wood, kokeshi are said to have been around since Japan's Edo period, from 1603–1867. Typically, the dolls have painted cylindrical, long bodies and round heads. The most traditional dolls have neither arms nor legs. Every kokeshi is different, and they've remained a popular souvenir for hundreds of years.

My first two kokeshi—a small boy and girl twin set with big grins and brightly colored bodies—were just that: souvenirs. Another gift from one of my father's trips, they're more of the "creative kokeshi" mold, as one of them is sporting a tiny wooden beret, and I can't imagine their maniacal smiles fit with tradition. I have three more, all clustered together in my living room, on a shelf beside the television. I hadn't ever given much thought to my kokeshi dolls or Japan's relationship with dolls in general until a Japanese friend visited and regaled my daughter and me will fantastical tales of superstition and history.

Dolls, according to Japanese lore, have souls and can even possess otherworldly abilities. Legend has it that an old doll that has been treasured and loved and passed down through generations can bring good luck to a childless couple trying to conceive. Soul-filled dolls are believed to bring other kinds of luck as well and offer protection to children.

The most cherished dolls are indeed the ones passed from generation to generation, especially in a set comprised of an emperor and empress, three court ladies, five musicians, two ministers, and three servants. In Japan, such dolls are considered heirlooms, as valuable as any antique. These dolls are used to celebrate the annual *Hinamatsuri*, the country's annual doll festival, held on Girls' Day. Every March 3, a family's Hinamatsuri dolls are displayed and prayers are offered for young girls' health and happiness.

I like the idea of Hinamatsuri dolls, and as much as I am loathe to admit it, I can relate to the notion of dolls with souls. This is completely at odds with my rational mind, but it's just that my dolls, well, my dolls always seem to be filled with so much personality. I know that I'm projecting these "personalities" upon them, and that my empathy for these cloth, plastic, and wooden toys is based on nothing close to logic, but still—there's something enchanting and real about them, and I couldn't bear to give them up.

In the West, such talk borders on the ramblings of a crazy doll lady, but in Japan, where dolls are honored and revered, my affinity for Blythe dolls and Dals and kokeshis would be normal, even tame. And if I ever found that I could no longer give my dolls the love and attention they deserved, I could take them to the yearly *Ningyo Kuyo* ceremony, held in Tokyo's Ueno Park every September.

Bunka doll, 2011. Handmade by the author

Hello, Cutie!

Ningyo Kuyo is a ritual funeral mass for unloved and neglected dolls. In keeping with the belief that dolls have souls, simply discarding one or throwing it away is a big no-no. Instead, people have the opportunity to bring them to the Ningyo Kuyo to be burned en masse under the blessing of a Shinto priest who prays for the dolls before the pile is set on fire.

I look at photographs from previous years' ceremonies and start to feel equally anxious and sad. I think of the large Tupperware bin of vintage dolls I have in storage and vow to find them a good home—but only after I can shake the images of burning dolls.

I wander into my daughter's bedroom in search of something distracting and cheery. I stop in front of her display of handmade *bunka* dolls; they're so cute and sweet-looking that I just have to smile. It wasn't long ago that I discovered bunka dolls and became completely beguiled. Like so much Japanese cute, the dolls' design is quite simple. Made of cloth with attached limbs, bunka dolls wear gathered dresses with a ribbon tied at the neck, bonnets with a short fringe of hair peeking out, and have hand-painted faces with big eyes and tiny bow-shaped mouths.

Over a period of a couple of months, I whipped up a dozen dolls using metallic stretch fabric in pastel colors instead of the traditional cotton. I thought I might try selling a few, but my daughter quickly claimed them and they were spirited to her room. I didn't have the heart to take them away. I'm not the only one who's drawn to the bunka doll. There's a coterie of crafters—both in Japan and the West—making new bunka dolls, and as more cute collectors are introduced to them, their popularity will surely grow.

Authentic vintage bunka dolls are rare and expensive. Translated, bunka doll means "culture doll," and got its start in the early twentieth century. Unlike kokeshi or the for-display-only Hinamatsuri dolls, bunkas were soft and designed to be played with and cuddled. The bunka is the Japanese equivalent to the American or English rag doll, only cuter. Play dolls are always hard to find in good shape, so it stands to reason that mint vintage bunkas are so elusive. Thankfully, many of today's cutest Japanese-style dolls are much easier to get your hands on—even if they aren't from Japan.

Everything about Momiji dolls seems Japanese: they're small (only three inches [7.5 cm] tall), have big round heads, and their basic clean design is clearly inspired by kokeshi dolls. They're known as "message dolls" and have cute hand-painted Asian faces. Turn them upside down and you'll find a secret note tucked up inside them. Yes, Momiji dolls have "Japanese" written all over them. The only thing is, Momiji HQ is actually in Henley in

Momiji dolls. Photo: Matej Lužnik ©Momiji

Arden, a small town in Warwickshire, England, population 2,100. What exactly is it about Momiji dolls that has the cute world so smitten—and how did an independent British company create a sensation with their Japanese-style dolls? I send a note off to Momiji creative director and co-founder Claire Rowlands.

Starting with twelve doll designs in 2005, the line now numbers close to 200 and is known for collaborating with artists worldwide and for the quirky personalities it assigns each of its dolls. "Our fans love the collectable aspect of the brand—they're kind of addictive," Claire says. "It's also fun to match Momiji dolls to your friends' personalities. Know someone who loves knitting and techno music? There's a Momiji that does too!"

Claire acknowledges the impact that Japanese style had on Momiji dolls but notes that as the brand has developed, so have its influences. "In the early days of Momiji, we were definitely influenced by our adventures in Tokyo and Seoul. As the brand has grown, we've worked with designers from all over the world. We have more of a global feel. Of course, we still have our roots in the stylized aesthetic of Japan, but there's always a strong dose of English eccentricity too."

Hello, Cutie!

The marriage of Japanese aesthetics and kooky English style has been a winning combination for Claire and the Momiji team, and serves as another example of the ongoing appeal of *kawaii*, the term most often used to define Japanese-style cute.

The kawaii aesthetic is something I'm all too familiar with. Collectors of every type of Japanese or Japanese-influenced doll—new or old—abound, but it's that big-eyed, Showa-era look that always gets me. And it's not just the dolls that I'm a sucker for. Perhaps the most influential mark on cute culture has been left by *shojo-ga* (translation: illustrations of girls). These innocent-looking, wide-eyed girly-girls started to appear in the late 1950s in the work of artist Makoto Takahashi, and books of his work—not to mention prints or originals—are cherished, rarely coming up for sale in the West.

Also known simply as "Macoto," Takahashi is widely considered the father of contemporary Japanese cute. His style is frequently mimicked, and his influence can be seen everywhere in cute-world, something I quickly discover when I start taking a closer look at his work. There's something dreamy about his illustrations of girls; they're almost ethereal with their soft features and sparkly eyes. I'm somewhat familiar with Takahashi's work—he's done many cover illustrations for the *Gothic & Lolita Bible*, a Japanese style "mook" (a magazine/book hybrid), and is featured in the book *Collector File, Vol. 1: Girls In Pop.* His illustrations have also graced the covers of notebooks and other merchandise, and he's illustrated many books in his long career.

Makoto Takahashi's work has had immeasurable effects on cute culture in general, but perhaps most obviously in modern manga and anime—especially those featuring young women as the central characters. My daughter's been hooked on manga and anime for the past couple of years. I've sat through umpteen battle scenes and marveled at the number of cross-dressing characters there seem to be. I've also decided that the subgenre of "magical girl" stories is a whole lot of cute-girl, ass-kicking fun.

Magical girls (or *mahou shoujo*) typically have, well, magical powers, often derived from a special object like a wand or piece of jewelry. Magical girls can transform into super-tough, nearly indestructible fighters and frequently have secret identities that must be kept from family and friends. Their stories often follow the tried-and-true convention of good-school-girl-by-day and slayer-of-evil-by-night.

Sally the Witch is regarded as the first magical-girl anime. Released in 1966, the series beat the original magical-girl manga, 1962's *Himitsu no Akko-chan*, to the screen by three years. The story followed the adventures of a princess witch called Sally who lived among mortals and had no clue of her real identity.

Madoka Magica Nendoroid anime figurine, China, 2011, ©Good Smile Company

Hello, Cutie!

She used her powers to fend off thieves, fight fires, and thwart crimes. That Sally shared traits with Samantha Stevens, the central character in the television show *Bewitched*, was not likely a coincidence, as *Bewitched* was a huge hit in Japan in the mid-1960s.

The 1970s saw magical girls start to do battle just like their *shonen* (boy) counterparts in *Cutie Honey*, which in 1973 was released as a manga and then as an anime series later that same year. In the West, magical girls didn't really hit mainstream consciousness until the early 1990s when *Sailor Moon* took the animation world by storm. This time, the magical girls' powers were designed exclusively for fighting evil, making the series unlike any of its predecessors.

You can see sparks of *Sally the Witch*, *Cutie Honey*, and *Sailor Moon* in many of today's magical-girl series, but the genre has taken another turn with the wildly popular *Puella Magi Madoka Magica*—or *Madoka Magica* for short. Madoka looks like the cutest little thing, with her pink pigtails and shy smile, but that's where the sweetness ends. *Madoka Magica's* plot revolves around regular girls who, in return for the granting of one wish, become magical girls responsible for not-so-cute issues like suicide and murder. It's not nearly as depressing as it sounds; somehow, the cuteness balances the darkness, and it works. Released in Japan in the spring of 2011, *Madoka Magica* was an instant hit and is credited with revitalizing the magical girl genre.

Madoka and her friends may have discovered that being a magical girl isn't all fun and games, but to their fans, dressing up like one certainly is. Whether it's Madoka in her adorable pink-and-white mini-skirted battle outfit, Sailor Moon in her sweet, schoolgirl-inspired dress, or a cuddly yellow Pikachu of Pokémon fame, dressing up as the cutest anime, manga, or video game characters in public raises nary an eyebrow in Japan.

Costume play—or cosplay as it's more commonly known—has been around for more than seventy years. Even in the late 1930s, science-fiction super-fans dressed up as their favorite characters and turned up at conventions in the United States. But it wasn't until the 1980s that cute cosplay started to gain momentum as reams of Japanese anime flooded into the West. Here, dressing up as your favorite anime character is usually an activity reserved for conventions and meets, but in Japan you can see cosplayers milling about on weekends in the Akihabara district of Tokyo and posing for pictures with tourists. The costumes are often intricate and loaded with detail. Some of them are commissioned from cosplay costume-makers, but frequently are homemade.

My daughter is not the most outgoing girl. She's by no means anti-social or painfully shy, but the fact that she wanted to dress up as the

Candy Candy anime character mask, 1970s

Hello, Cutie!

cute Pokémon trainer May to attend her first anime convention came as a surprise. We studied stills from the television show, noting the details of her outfit, and I got to work.

I'd never attended anything even remotely similar to an anime con before. Sure, I'd seen photos of people dressed up in crazy costumes and masks, carrying faux weapons. It was out of my realm of my experience, and even though I've been curious about Japanese popular culture much of my life, attending such an event had never really crossed my mind. But there we were on a Sunday at a university campus, my daughter dressed as a Pokémon trainer and me and her step-dad in conspicuously "normal" attire. The enthusiasm of the 5,000-odd attendees was infectious, and the overall friendliness and lack of cynicism refreshing. Best of all was the vendors' hall with rows of makeshift booths filled with all sorts of Asian imports, from big-eyed Pullip and Dal dolls to plush toys and cute, miniature figurines in blind boxes (you don't know which figure you'll get until you open the box). I remember thinking that it was worth the price of admission just for the shopping, and I knew that it was only a matter of time before we were back at another convention.

Make that two months. The summer trip we planned happened to coincide with another anime con, so there was another costume to make. This time, my daughter wanted the costume of one of the cute antique dolls from (my personal favorite anime), *Rozen Maiden*. Five months later, there was another convention and another costume—a different doll from *Rozen Maiden*. Now she has her sights set on being Madoka from *Madoka Magica*.

Anime characters aren't the only Japanese imports to get the cosplay treatment. Step foot in any Japanese pop culture convention or festival and you're bound to see dozens of girls clad in ruffled, pastel-colored dresses, knee socks, and Mary Janes milling about holding lace parasols and looking as cute as can be. These are the Sweet Lolita girls, and their world is a pretty pink paradise. Gothic Lolita girls wear similar get-ups, but in black, and have darkly lined eyes and powder-pale skin.

I've long been intrigued by the Lolitas, and confess to having bought copies of their periodical guide-to-life, *Gothic & Lolita Bible*, every time I come across one. These books are rare here, and of course, written entirely in Japanese. The now sadly defunct American publisher Tokyopop published five editions in English that are worth tracking down for every wannabe Lolita or curious voyeur like myself, and provide wonderful insight into the Lolita lifestyle.

I know from my secret indulgence (i.e., my stash of *Gothic & Lolita Bibles*) that, beyond the puffy dresses and hair bows, etiquette and tea parties also play a role in the Lolita world, but

Victoria Suzanne decked out in full Lolita gear.
Photo: Kayla Lukes

I'm no means an expert, so it's time to speak with someone who is. Victoria Suzanne is a university student and Lolita blogger living in small-town Connecticut. I happened upon her site *parfaitdoll.com* by chance and was promptly fascinated by her commitment to Lolita and her pretty pastel-colored wardrobe. "I was a junior in high school [in 2008] doing a history project when I stumbled onto the Japanese movie *Kamikaze Girls*, which features a Lolita as the main character," Victoria says. "At first I was just curious, but after seeing more I was immediately in love. Most girls describe seeing the clothes and having a moment of being instantly smitten. In *Kamikaze Girls*, they liken it to a metaphorical bullet to the heart."

Victoria explains that while makeup and dresses are key to being a Lolita, it goes beyond fashion. "[The] lifestyle is about bringing all the things I love about Lolita—attention to detail, pretty shades of pink, and a fairy-tale feel—into my everyday life. While a lot of it is something simple, like drinking my usual morning tea from a cute teacup instead of, say, my dad's #1 Tennis Player mug, it's also about how I choose to live my life. I try to take good care of my appearance even when I'm not in Lolita clothes. I listen to music with Lolita sentiments, but most importantly, I try to behave like a princess or lady would—polite, neat, kind, and charming."

And while some critics say that Sweet Lolitas dress like cupcakes and deride them

Hello, Cutie!

as silly if not downright anti-feminist, Lolitas like Victoria have a different take on what this lifestyle represents. "I think a girl or woman of any age wants to feel like a princess or an elegant lady, and Lolita [fashions] provide that feeling and confidence much more than today's mainstream fashions do," she says. "People who know me accept it and even enjoy my look. My family and friends are curious to see what I'll wear next, and often strangers will compliment me on the street. Even when I am wearing casual Lolita style and no makeup, passersby will tell me the look is pretty. I think they like it, as it's so fresh and feminine and not the usual jeans and T-shirt."

Lolitas are not just girls playing dress-up; in Japan, Lolita Girls have been employed by the government as official Ambassadors of Cute, a controversial program launched in March 2009 to promote tourism by Japan's Ministry of Foreign Affairs. Known officially as Trend Communicators of Japanese Pop Culture, the appointed *Kawaii Taishi* joined Hello Kitty, who was named Japan's tourism and ambassador to China and Hong Kong in 2008, and Doraemon, the anime cat who was made "cartoon culture ambassador" that same year.

From Brazil and Thailand to fashion capitals Paris and New York, the three Ambassadors of Cute traveled the globe promoting Japanese cute. There was singer-actress Yu Kimura, whose look reflected the oft-copied street style found in Harajuku, Tokyo's hub

A peek inside Victoria Suzanne's wardrobe.
Photo: Kayla Lukes

of youth culture. There was fashion designer Shizuka Fujioka, who dresses in her own interpretation of the traditional Japanese schoolgirl uniform, and there was Misako Aoki, a well-known Lolita model who has worked for top Lolita fashion brands like Baby, the Stars Shine Bright. Of the three, it was Misako Aoki who was photographed, interviewed, and talked about the most. Dressed like a Victorian doll in fairy-tale dresses, Aoki charmed crowds and signed autographs. Of the three types of Cute Ambassadors, the girl in the petticoats and bows was the most interesting? Relatable? Non-threatening? Aoki garnered heaps of media attention; subsequently, so did the Lolita look and the Ambassador of Cute program. But it soon became clear that not everyone was happy with the Lolitas or the Cute campaign at all.

Critics questioned the message sent by the Japanese government's appointment of three young women portraying what some would assert are negative female stereotypes. They argued that in particular, Aoki the Lolita and Fujioka the schoolgirl were encouraging the infantilization of women, while at the same time presenting a sexualized image of them. The pop culture world's relationship with Lolitas is complex and polarized, and opinions range from those who think they are anti-feminist or perverse to the people who find the Lolita style cute, harmless, and innocent.

I grab a copy of one of my *Gothic & Lolita Bibles* and flip through it, wondering why I find it so interesting—it's not like I'm going to start dressing like a Lolita any time soon. I ask my daughter what she thinks, as she occasionally likes to dress in vintage Lolita-style dresses to play around the house, and like me enjoys pouring over issues of Lolita magazines or "mooks."

"It's pretty," she says with a shrug. Maybe it is that simple, and the appeal is purely aesthetic for me: the over-the-top dresses with vintage twists; the fashion spreads shot at historic, Gothic estates or set among lush greenery. For me, Lolita is a candy-coated fantasy, removed from reality and sexual politics. It's fashion at its cutest, and a continually growing faction of Japanese cool.

Inside Japan's Magical Pop Culture Kingdom

Patrick W. Galbraith

Understanding and untangling the complexities Japanese pop culture is daunting task, but one that American writer and researcher, Patrick W. Galbraith, has eagerly embraced. A PhD candidate at Duke University and the author of *The Otaku Encyclopedia, Tokyo Realtime: Akihabara* and *Otaku Spaces*, Patrick spent his formative years in Alaska and Montana, where he learned to read and write Japanese in high school. But by then his fascination with Japanese culture had already taken root.

"When I was about five or six, I saw my older brothers watching this cartoon, which looked like nothing I had ever seen before. It was all sci-fi and hard-edged and adult and cool," he explains. "It seemed so different and so deep, something beyond the ability of a kid who didn't speak the language or know about the world to comprehend. I got totally hooked."

Patrick W. Galbraith dressed as Goku from the anime Dragon Ball Z on the streets of Akihabara.
Photo: Max Hodges

Anime was the gateway to Patrick's professional studies: he studied at the University of Tokyo and now splits his time between Duke University in North Carolina and Japan. Anime remains a passion, and he harbors particular affection for *bishōjo* anime—which feature beautiful girl characters—and the magical-girl genre. "I get so involved in anime that I forget where [I am] and who I am. There is one scene in *Sailor Moon* where the protagonist, Usagi, has just been dumped by her boyfriend and collapses in a phone booth, sobbing uncontrollably. I was so moved! Tears streaming down my face, man. Seriously. And I hated her boyfriend so much—I could have killed him...if he were a real person."

Such intense reaction and emotional involvement in anime, manga, or video games is not unusual among fans both in Japan and abroad. A word that's frequently bandied about and perhaps too often incorrectly defined or overused is *otaku*. Since Patrick—quite literally—wrote the book on otaku culture, he's the ideal person to help me understand it better.

"[An otaku is] someone who is serious about his or her hobbies, typically manga, anime, and games, which reflects the interests of the fandom as it emerged in Japan in the 1970s and 1980s. The most common definition of otaku is people who are narrow and deep in their interests—something like a hardcore or cult fan—but this doesn't really apply to fandom in a networked age. There is so much information and media out there that no one can master everything, so people are wide and shallow in their interests," Patrick says.

"I think that otaku today are people who are actively engaged in their fandom," he continues. "They have to be networked with others to get all the information they want. They need to straddle and curate flows of information, making meaning out of the deluge. Otaku today probably consume more media than they did in the 1970s and 1980s, though perhaps they do not pay for it or spend a lot

of time with specific products. Instead, they might produce fanworks or cosplay or write a blog about anime. This reflects an intense interest that continues over a long period of time, which I think is the correct approach to otaku. It is not a definition, because otaku is a qualitative, not quantitative, issue. At a time when anime, manga, and games are commonplace, otaku are people who love [them] in an entirely uncommon way."

Cover of *The Otaku Encyclopedia* by Patrick W. Galbraith. Image courtesy of Kodansha International

Hello, Cutie!

All the Pretty Girls

Cynthia Flores

Photo: School Portrait Studios

Cynthia Flores has been enamored with illustrated, big-eyed Japanese girls since childhood. Growing up in the American territory of Guam, she remembers her mother taking her to a shop to buy shoes, but it wasn't the shoes that Cynthia remembers most fondly. The store also sold all sorts of cute Japanese imports like stationery, pencil cases, and purses featuring images of girly anime characters Candy Candy, Lady Oscar, Marie Antoinette, Lalabel, and Sandybelle. This early introduction fueled Cynthia's life-long love of the retro, big-eyed aesthetic.

Both a collector and dealer (she often sells items on Etsy and eBay), Cynthia hasn't always found quick acceptance of her hobby. "When I was a teenager, my mother told me I was too old to be collecting dolls," she says. "I tried for a few years not to collect dolls and 'grow up,' but I couldn't. I found myself still looking at many cute doll or toy items, even after having my own children."

Her collection today centers around the items featuring artwork by Makoto Takahashi, Masako Watanabe, or Eico Hanamura, and other artists from the early era of shōjo manga. And it's no surprise that it's those items that have become her bestsellers. "The pencil cases with any of the anime or retro-girl art from [those] artists [sell best]. When I put up popular brands like Margaret, Sunstar, Colleen, or Venice, they get snatched up within a few hours."

A former educator who is currently a stay-at-home mom, Cynthia has adopted an admirable philosophy when it comes to dealing with the at times conflicting roles of collector and seller. "Quite often I decide to let go of many of my beloved treasures in the hope that someone will enjoy their beauty as much as I did. I've found it much easier to let go of something when I think of how much pleasure it will give to someone else," she says.

Always upbeat when it comes to her affection for Japanese cute, Cynthia also has plenty of encouraging words for long-time collectors and newbies who can find sourcing collectable gems frustrating: "[However] rare an item may be, it is possible to find it. I thought I would never, ever see particular items…but they do show up in the usual places like eBay, Etsy, or Yahoo! Japan auctions. One just needs to be diligent, and patience works to your advantage. Just don't think it's impossible, because anything is possible—with time!"

LiveJournal: ggsdolls.livejournal.com/
Blog: ggsdolls.blogspot.com/
Etsy: etsy.com/shop/ggsdolls

Cynthia Flores' favorite item from her collection, a Glico Badge/Pin of Himeko, a character from the manga series *Ohayo Himeko* by Eico Fujiwara.
Photos: Cynthia Flores

Items from Cynthia Flores' collection of cute dolls, toys, and novelties

Hello, Cutie!

I Want Candy

*F*ood is innately sensual—if not downright sexual at times—and sweets occupy a special place on the food-sex continuum, often pairing the innocent and the erotic. Pastel colors and bold primaries remind us of childhood, and rounded shapes soften our emotions. Our brains and bodies crave the impending sugar rush on sight. Candy and other treats are the come-hither coquettes of the food world: ever-teasing, always tempting, and forever daring us to succumb to our naughty urges.

I'm no different than any other cute-food lover. I've been seduced by fanciful cupcakes and had my wallet opened by packages of teensy-weensy plastic Japanese food miniatures. I've been to a Katy Perry concert with my daughter and marveled at her marketing smarts, marrying her bouncy persona with candy-coated imagery and sex. I've also eaten too many things I probably shouldn't because they were simply too cute and yummy to resist. Such indulgence is nothing new—sugar has been around since 1200 BCE, after all—but as with fashions, our preferred styles of sweets change. And though the aesthetic appeal of sweets has always been important, the reign of cute food is very much a modern trend, and the appetite for candies and cupcakes shows no sign of waning.

Shops selling old-fashioned and upscale candy are on the rise thanks to the success of ventures like Dylan Lauren's New York-based candy empire, Dylan's Candy Bar. With seven American locations and a booming web business, Lauren purveys goods featuring candy images, including iPhone covers, notebooks, and an ice-cream cone knitted hat.

But when I visit the Candy Bar, what I want most of all are the Candy Spill rain boots, white rubber galoshes with pictures of lollipops, jelly beans, and licorice ropes all seemingly tumbling down the calf and foot. I'm even

Pinypon figurine, China, 2011, ©Famosa-Spain

Hello, Cutie!

more excited when I noticed that they carry the same style for kids, but then remember that my daughter wouldn't be caught dead walking with her mother in matching rain boots. She would be more than happy, however, to share a bag of yummy bulk candies, or even better, a cupcake. Because as fun and cute as candy can be, it's the once-lowly cupcake that has taken center stage in the last decade. Cupcakes are the consummate cute food.

We all remember that episode of *Sex and the City* in which Carrie meets Miranda for a chat and a cupcake at Magnolia Bakery. The scene was short but its impact immeasurable. Since it aired in 2000, countless cupcake vendors have popped up in cities across North America, over 300 cupcake cookbooks have been published, and reality television shows like *Cupcake Wars, Cupcake Sisters*, and *Cupcake Girls* have aired. The original Magnolia Bakery—a West Village institution since 1996—has become a popular New York tourist destination, shipping cupcakes coast-to-coast in the US and selling cupcake-themed garments such as T-shirts and aprons through its website.

As a child in the 1970s, I remember the birthday parties, Betty Crocker cake mixes, and the colored frosting and confetti-like sprinkles that made cupcakes so appealing; cupcakes were for kids and they didn't even register on the radar of the burgeoning fusion-foodie culture of the 1980s and 1990s.

But today, cupcakes are universal—appealing to kids and urban sophisticates alike—and there is something in cupcake culture for everyone. There are zombie cupcakes, cupcake competitions, cupcake calendars, and an entire Martha Stewart recipe book devoted to cupcakes. They can be personalized, made-to-order, and decorated so beautifully that it's impossible to take a bite without experiencing a twinge of guilt.

That guilt is precisely what I'm feeling as I gawk at the chocolate cheesecake cupcakes in the display case at my local cupcake store, Buttercream Bake Shoppe. I'm here to challenge owner Toni Morberg to create the cutest cupcakes she can for me. Toni and her team are game, and I'm curious what she'll come up with. Everyone has their own interpretation of cute, and it's no different in the cupcake world. I've seen snowman cupcakes, cupcakes with pastel-colored rainbows, and winky-face cupcakes—even intricate Sesame Street and Disney character cupcakes—so I can't wait to see what Toni will have concocted for me when I go back to her shop in a couple of weeks.

After my initial meeting with Toni, I get to thinking more about the cupcake-cuteness connection: they're small, many of us associate them with childhood, and they can be decorated in an endless number of cute ways. I wonder if it was always this way. There's some-

Wind-up piggy bank, Hong Kong, 1970s

Hello, Cutie!

thing about cupcakes that's innately retro, in a mid-twentieth-century housewife-in-a-floral-day-dress-baking-for-her-family kind of way. They strike me as one of those all-American inventions, a novelty at their introduction, maybe a newfangled way to sell muffin tins. While most of my suppositions are wrong, I did get one thing right: cupcakes are indeed American, at least by name. The first use of the term is credited to Eliza Leslie, who wrote instructions for "cup cakes" in her 1828 book *Seventy-Five Receipts for Pastry, Cakes, and Sweetmeats.* But the baking of small individual-serving cakes goes back to the late eighteenth century and Amelia Simmons' book *American Cookery,* published in 1796. Small fruitcakes called "Queen Cakes" had been baked in England, and these were likely the inspiration for the American single-serving "cup cake," though there's no way to know for sure.

As for the name, there are two theories as to how it originated: one, it was a reference to the measure used to make a "cup cake"—one cup; two, that they were first baked in actual cups, as the muffin tin didn't appear until the nineteenth century. According to New Jersey-based librarian and food historian Lynne Olver, whose website *foodtimeline.org* has been the go-to source for food reference since 1999, there is evidence to support both arguments, and the etymology of the word "cupcake" remains a mystery.

A selection of cupcakes in the window at Buttercream Bake Shoppe

Two weeks later, and feeling much more educated about the history of cupcakes, I'm back at the Buttercream Bake Shoppe to see what Toni and her staff have made. They've interpreted cute in several different ways. "We thought kittens were cute, and the 'soda shop' cupcake is a classic. Then there's the garden theme in celebration of spring," Toni explains, going through the thought process behind all of the creation of the cupcakes. I'm personally partial to the "soda shop" cupcake with the robin's egg-blue icing, colorful sprinkles, and maraschino cherry on top. It practically

I Want Candy

Ceramic owl cookie jar, Japan, 1970s

Hello, Cutie!

screams cute, though I couldn't be more pleased with all of Toni's creations.

Back at home, I simply have to treat myself to one of the half-dozen cupcakes I've brought back with me from Buttercream. "It's a treat that looks as good as it tastes," Toni had said at the shop, and she couldn't have been more right. Stuffed and giddy, I try to settle down at my desk. I squirm and readjust my position, but can't concentrate, so I log on to Etsy, my favorite procrastination website, for a bit of virtual window-shopping disguised as work. I type "cupcake" into the search box and am stunned when nearly 100,000 items come up— and that's only in the "handmade" category.

I scroll through a few pages, finding cupcake greeting cards, crocheted plush cupcakes, and adorable gingham-print cupcake wrappers, but very few actual cupcakes. There are plenty of shops selling very real-looking fake cupcakes, with ingredients like spackle, polymer clay, and expansion foam standing in for flour, sugar, and eggs. Who buys fake cupcakes? I am admittedly perplexed, so I send a quick message to Shimrit Hamsi of Shimrita Cupcakes. She has sold more than 2,000 since opening her online shop in August 2009, and explains the appeal of her faux confections this way: "Most of my customers are photographers who use the cupcakes as photo props for birthday sessions and mothers who buy the cupcakes for birthday decorations."

The yummy results of Buttercream Bake Shoppe's cute cupcake challenge

The fake cupcake thing is starting to make a bit more sense when Shimrit says they are mostly used as props and decoration. But that's not to say that the former lawyer doesn't get her share of odd looks when she tells people about her business. "I really don't know how to explain to people what I do," she says. "I tell them that I make fake cupcakes and cakes and they look at me and say, 'So the cakes that you make are not for eating?' They think they didn't hear me correctly ... [I explain that the cupcakes] are for display or for photo props, and they look at me as if I were crazy."

Candy Village Shop from the Re-ment Puchi Petite Candy House Collection, China, 2008, ©Re-Ment Co., Ltd.

Hello, Cutie!

Shimrit's customers know that she's far from crazy, and once I take a closer look at her line—which now includes fake cupcake jewelry boxes, cupcake hair bands, and clever cupcake door knobs—I find myself imagining different ways to use them in my photography work. The cupcake hair band would look especially cute for a photo of my daughter. But that will have to wait—there are more cute fake foods to investigate, all of which look good enough to eat.

Drop the name Re-ment to any Barbie or Blythe doll collector, and they're sure to light up with excitement. Producers of highly detailed Puchi Petites 1:6 scale miniatures, many of which are food, the Japanese company's wares are sold in "blind" boxes or plastic pouches, which basically means you don't know which part of the set you are getting until you open it.

This makes collecting Re-ment simultaneously fun and frustrating. I was hoping for the meat-carving station set of the Hotel Buffet collection when I happened upon a stash of Re-ment at a local toy shop, but wasn't disappointed one bit with the fruit-and-juice set I got, with its tiny melon slices and an impeccably crafted (miniature) handful of ripe red strawberries. Sure, you can buy opened boxes online and know exactly what you're getting, but sometimes a blind box is far more fun and provokes a nostalgic anticipation, like

Shimrit Hamsi's fake cupcake creations.
Photo: Shimrit Hamsi

that feeling you had as a kid plugging quarters into a toy-filled vending machine at the mall or digging through a box of cereal to see which one of the prizes depicted on the back of the box was yours.

Occasionally, there's a series you simply fall in love with and have to have, and sometimes you even have the luck of a local find. Shopping in Chinatown with my daughter one day, I was delighted to discover an unopened display box of the discontinued Minnie Mouse Lovely Cakes set, which meant all eight sets were included, and our Blythe and Dal dolls could now enjoy plastic cakes and pies served up on the most precious red-and-white polka dot plates.

Iwako puzzle erasers, 2011, China

Hello, Cutie!

I think it's impossible for any cute collector to resist Re-ment, whether they're using it to add detail to dioramas or as props for doll photography, or whether they buy it simply to marvel at the teeny-tiny perfection that the company has become known for since it launched its first Puchi Petites food series, Japanese Meals, in 2002. That Re-ment and its main mini-food-making rivals, Megahouse and Orcara, hail from Japan comes as no surprise. A small country with an inherent lack of space, Japan is the natural place to produce small, efficient, and practical products. And given the Japanese aesthetic penchant for all things childlike, it's also the natural place to produce small, super-cute, whimsical products.

Take the puzzle eraser business, for instance. (That there is a puzzle eraser business in Japan is a statement on its own.) Since 1985, the stationery company Iwako has been selling *omoshiro keshigomu* (translation: "funny erasers"). Often referred to as omokeshi, the brightly colored erasers can be pulled apart and the pieces interchanged. Many are in the shapes of food—mostly sweets. Take an ice cream piece and place it on a burger bun or create your own half-sushi, half-cake combo. The possibilities grow with the number you collect, something I know well from watching my daughter and her friends collect and trade the novelty erasers, which are rarely used for actual erasing.

Iwako produces about 150,000 erasers per day, and if you visit the company's Official Japanese Eraser Museum (*erasermuseum. com*), you'll find photos of an astounding 814 different erasers, from the French Pastry set to Dream Bananas. You'll also find Dream Erasers produced by Zensinsyoji, Iwako's main competitor. But it's all friendly competition, it seems; the companies are run separately, each by one of two brothers.

Set me in front of a pile of omokeshi and it's unlikely I could tell you which ones are Iwako and which ones are Zensinsyoji. I might be able to discern the knock-off made-in-China ones that have flooded the market in recent years, but the differences between those produced by the two made-in-Japan companies are lost on me. Not so with serious puzzle eraser collectors and dealers—like the omokeshi sellers and bloggers at *sausalitoferry.com*—who will tell you that Zensinsyoji erasers tend to be smaller than Iwako's and incorporate more pastel colors.

Japanese food-related cute runs the gamut from the populist to esoteric. Puzzle erasers can be bought at toy shops, novelty stores, and Walmarts all over North America; finding the more obscure character lines produced by Japan's San-X can be a greater challenge. The chief competitor of Sanrio, San-X characters are decidedly more odd, often weaving darkly humorous background stories into their

Clown cup, USA, 1950s, ©Tastee-Freez

Hello, Cutie!

profiles. San-X designers also have a penchant for putting faces on the most mundane items and spinning a story around them. Like Tissue-San, for example, a box of, yes, tissues, who hangs out with a roll of toilet paper. San-X also promotes characters that are food with a face.

San-X experienced moderate success in Japan's character goods market back in the late 1980s with Pinny-Mu, a cute, simply drawn bear. But it wasn't until 1995 when the flat, lazy panda called Tarepanda was introduced that the company really started to garner international attention from cute enthusiasts. To date, San-X has rolled out more than fifty characters, including my personal favorites the Cheese Family, and Beer Chan, a happy-go-lucky yellow fairy who always has a frosty pint in his hands.

I discovered Beer Chan and the Cheese Family in 2003 on a shopping expedition with my writer friend Jeremy to Richmond, British Columbia's Yaohan Center. In one of Yaohan's gift shops, I found Beer Chan notebooks and a Cheese Family pencil case. After shopping and back in Vancouver's West End, Jeremy and I both wanted to know more about these unusual characters and stopped in at a big computer shop to see what we could find out online. What we hit upon was truly bizarre. It was strange enough that Beer Chan is a fairy, but the Cheese Family's family tree was

unbelievable. Yet there they were: the architect Emmental father and housewife soft-cheese mom; the boys: the oldest, Chi-Brother, a former triad gang leader with a dollop of cream on his head, shy Plain, cowardly Blueberry, and the youngest, Cream, who idolizes Chi-Brother. There are three girls in the family as well: tomboy Cranberry, spoiled Nuts, and Baby Cheese. And we can't forget the older generation: grandpa Blue Cheese and grandma Yogurt who, according to the San-X Cheese Family biographies, has poor blood circulation and likes to knit. So spectacular was this find that we felt compelled to set all of the store's computers to the Cheese Family web page (*rmlicensing.com/ENG/Sanx/cheesefamily.htm*) for others to encounter and enjoy.

The eccentric characters of San-X somehow seem more spirited than their Sanrio counterparts, and clearly inspire silliness in people like me. Their backstories and quirky personalities have certainly contributed to the company's growing success and market share. Perhaps it's that we can all relate more to the neuroses of these characters or maybe the appeal is in their unabashed kookiness. Alternately, we just may like food with a face on it—like one of San-X's most peculiar characters, Kogepan. The official story goes like this:

"Kogepan was supposed [to be] a high quality red bean bun with Hokkaido red bean filling, and it was limited to twenty pieces per day.

Gingerbread Man Dream Doll, Taiwan, 1970s, ©R. Dakin

Hello, Cutie!

However, it was over-baked at the bakery one day and it became apathetic. Its eyes turned into white and lack of expression on face [sic]. It's [sic] life changed at that moment, and it became a sad little bun with a pessimistic view of life. Sometimes, Kogepan is positive, but the passion never lasts long and fades away quickly."

Yes, Kogepan is a chronically depressed, burnt bean bun. But that's not to say he doesn't have friends, in spite of his sour disposition. There are always several upbeat, smiling breads in the bakery to keep him company, most notably, Kuriimupan (cream bread), Ichigopan (strawberry bread), Sumipan (charcoal bread), who's burned even more badly than Kogepan, and the Kireipan (pretty bread), the young, perfect breads.

The Kireipan figure prominently in the third episode of the Kogepan animated series produced in 2001. The four-minute short film shows Kogepan terrifying the giggly, innocent breads with stories of their likely fate after leaving the bakery (they will be cut in half and toasted) and then gets them drunk on milk—which is what breads apparently drink to get drunk—much to the chagrin of the baker.

The entire Kogepan experience is surreal, as are many of the stories used to sell children's toys and character merchandise. Kogepan may occupy a spot on the extreme side of weird, but even mainstream American cartoon characters have their quirks—though one might have to dig through layers of marketing propaganda to find them.

Many of the most memorable kids' characters were found primarily in books and films and on television until the 1970s, when the scope of marketing to children widened and media merged, creating a larger merchandising machine that sought to capture kids' attention and their parents' money by employing a multi-tiered consumer assault, tying in books with toys with television shows. The 1970s and early 1980s saw the birth of branding and licensing as we know it today. Leading the way were companies like American Greetings—which had great success with the first licensed character Holly Hobbie starting in 1974. Keen for another big hit, an illustration of a mop-topped rag doll with a calico strawberry-print bonnet was plucked from the greeting card department in 1977 (though she did not appear on cards until after the character's launch). She was given the full merchandising treatment and launched into the competitive industry in 1980. By the end of that year Strawberry Shortcake was a full-fledged star, with games, toys, a television special, and of course, those scented dolls.

The sweet-smelling dolls proved to be big business: toy licensee Kenner sold forty-five million of them in the first five years of production. Not since *Star Wars* had the

Strawberry Shortcake doll, Hong Kong, 1979, ©American Greeting Corporation

Hello, Cutie!

toy business seen such a profitable line, and naturally, a slew of imitators swamped the market, including my favorite, the 1981 set of Cooky Box Dolls, which were a cross between Strawberry Shortcake and late-1960s/early '70s sensation, Flatsy—dolls that were made of a rubbery plastic and only about one-quarter-inch (six-mm) thick. Cooky Box Dolls and other Strawberry imitators like Lil Lollypops and Jelly Beans Dolls didn't last long. But more than thirty years since its inception, Strawberry Shortcake is still going strong.

When Strawberry Shortcake sales dwindled in the late 1980s and then disappeared, it wasn't long before a newly made-over doll emerged in an attempt to capture the hearts of a whole new generation of consumers. Miss Shortcake has, over the years, undergone no less than four complete makeovers, first in 1991 and 2003, then in 2006 and 2009, respectively. Each time, her look changed somewhat, to the point that the current version is more Bratz doll than rag doll, with her short, short skirts and big, anime-style eyes. And while there are constant pals like Orange Blossom and Blueberry Muffin, it's hard not to notice that other characters have come and gone. Remember Strawberry's horse, Maple Stirrup, and his carriage, the Oatsmobile? Didn't think so. How about Café Olé, her friend from Mexicocoa? Not likely, unless you're a die-hard fan.

Fans are also sure to notice that one of Strawberry's long-time friends, Raspberry Tart, has been renamed Raspberry *Torte*, much to the dismay of many Shortcake collectors and purists. Collecting vintage Strawberry Shortcake items has been growing in popularity. It's an accessible hobby for doll enthusiasts. Since there were so many products produced, there is a lot of second-hand merchandise for sale, and much of it at reasonable prices. Still, I've always seen Strawberry Shortcake and her gang as harmless, cute, yet sort-of bland characters, concerned primarily with cleaning, baking, and other household chores I don't want to do (or watch animated characters do, no matter how cute).

I was in junior high by the time the first wave of Strawberry Shortcake-mania took hold, and fancied myself much too old (and much too cool) to do anything but laugh and roll my eyes when the commercials promoting the television special *Strawberry Shortcake: Housewarming Surprise* came on. Maybe there's something I'm missing, so I get in touch with UK-based Strawberry Shortcake fan Jane Pierrepont, who not only collects the dolls, she gives vintage SSC dolls—as they're known to insiders—makeovers and designs and makes clothes and patterns for the scented cuties that she sells worldwide through her Etsy shop.

Jane wasn't a 'Cake collector as a kid, and didn't dive into the sweet-smelling world of

Liddle Kiddles Sweet Treats Ice Cream Sundae dollhouse, Philippines, 1978, ©Mattel

Hello, Cutie!

Rose, Jane Pierrepont's favorite Strawberry
Shortcake doll, pre-makeover. Photo: Jane Pierrepont

Rose, Jane Pierrepont's favorite Strawberry
Shortcake doll, post-makeover. Photo: Jane Pierrepont

Strawberry Shortcake until after she kicked
off her grown-up doll collection with a Blythe
doll in 2007. From there, it was a slippery slope
that led to Dal dolls, a Moof, a Heroic Rendez-
vous doll, a Susie Sad Eyes doll and, of course,
Strawberry Shortcake and her friends. Her first
doll was a vintage Raspberry Tart, and that one
remains her favorite. Jane also prefers the older
dolls to the new. "My favorites are the Kenner
originals. The newer versions are sweet, but
they don't quite have the simple happiness that
the early ones have," she says.

Strawberry Shortcake dolls are markedly
less expensive than many vintage dolls, and
this likely contributes to their growing appeal.
When Jane Pierrepont was searching for a doll

One of Jane Pierrepont's Strawberry Shortcake designs, The Monster Sweater. Photo: Jane Pierrepont

to make clothes for and couldn't afford another Blythe, she found inspiration in the 'Cakes. "I searched on eBay for cheap vintage dolls and there she was—my little Raspberry Tart vintage Strawberry Shortcake! I felt little again and excited about making clothes; I loved their little faces and big feet—they made me happy. Straight away I started designing for my new addition," she recalls. "I used to make doll clothes all the time when I was little—Strawberry Shortcake [gave] me back the enthusiasm I had as a child."

Nostalgia plays an important role in cute culture, including the world of scented Strawberry Shortcake dolls, and this makes it easier for me to understand their appeal. As I browse through Jane's website checking out her adorable creations, the dolls look tempting to me. And she's right about the originals being cuter than the newer versions. The 1980s wasn't so very long ago, I think, but there's a wistfulness that comes over me when I look at Strawberry Shortcake's freckled face and extra-big forehead. My mind immediately jumps to the cliché of "innocence"—I'm loathe to type the word, but that's what it is—that best describes the benign little fruity gal I never understood. I imagine her as calm and perennially happy. I suspect Jane would agree with my assessment. She describes her experiences with SSC dolls as bringing out her youth—the way all the best cute does. "I only have to hold one in my hand, and I feel like a little girl again; it makes all my worries fade away for a bit."

Hello, Cutie!

The Queen of Cute Cuisine

BENTO BOX GURU CRYSTAL WATANABE MARRIES CUTE WITH NUTRITION

Crystal Watanabe

Photo: Stefanie Sakamoto

A traditional bento is a Japanese all-in-one meal. The bento box is that super-smart, shallow tray with section dividers that keeps your *kushiage* from your *tempura* from your *sashimi* or *gyoza*. Almost every Japanese restaurant offers some variation of bento boxes for their customers' convenience, but chances are the ones you've seen at your neighborhood sushi bar aren't nearly as cute as Crystal Watanabe's.

Born and raised in Hawaii, Crystal first discovered the cute side of bento while searching for an example of a typical bento to show a friend. "When I saw the images [of cute bento] on Google, I thought, I should do that!" she recalls.

Considering the Japanese penchant for cute and the long history of the bento—early versions of bento have been noted as far back as the Kamakura Period (1185–1333)—it's no wonder that the two should fuse for a feast that's as adorable-looking as it is nutritious.

In Japan, you'll find "character bento," featuring food designed to resemble popular characters from manga and anime, as well as elaborate "picture bento," in which the food is crafted to look like everything from people to architecture. Crystal Watanabe specializes in bento that's decidedly cute. She documents her ideas and designs on her blog, *aibento.net*, and her cookbook (with Maki Ogawa), *Yum-Yum Bento Box: Fresh Recipes for Adorable Lunches* is filled with darling tips, tricks, and recipes for making the cutest bentos.

A self-confessed perfectionist, Crystal carefully composes each element of her bento designs, taking inspiration from a variety of sources. "Usually I'll just come up with a subject to do with a holiday or something that's happened in my life and then start thinking about how I could recreate it with food. My brain churns and churns until I figure out the 'puzzle' of what foods to use," she says.

Those "puzzles" can consist of everything from smiley bears or flowers cut from cheese to a "fluffy lamb" made of pink cooked rice, a hard-boiled egg, a bit of ketchup, a piece of nori (seaweed), and a slice of cheese. Sounds simple, right? Trust me, it's not. But using Crystal's book, it doesn't take too long to get the hang of it—and having the right tools helps. "I love my nori punches the most," Crystal says. "The worst part of my first bento year was figuring out how to cut out little eyes and mouths. Now, with the punches, it's all really easy."

It's an exercise in perfection and perseverance. As Crystal says, "Making cute bento can be really tough at the start, but eventually you find a groove and become efficient at it. It just takes a bit of practice!"

· ·

Blog: fictionalfood.net
Blog: www.aibento.net
Twitter: @pikko

The cover of Crystal Watanabe and Maki Ogawa's book, *Yum-Yum Bento Box*. Photo: Maki Ogawa/ Quirk Books

Sugar Rush

Missy Munday

Photo: Missy Munday

As an out-and-proud fan and friend, it's hard to know where to start when discussing Missy Munday's creations. The Canadian mother of two who works under the moniker Boopsie Daisy, Missy is known in cute culture circles for her fantastical photographs, in which vintage doll heads often find themselves immersed in a bowl of Froot Loops or dripping with syrup atop a stack of pancakes. Incorporating food with vintage toys and dolls in curious ways is her trademark, along with punchy colors and a cheeky sense of humor.

Missy's aesthetic preferences were honed at an early age, as she spent weekends as a child snooping through her antiques salesman father's stash. "[When] I was about seven, I can remember coming across a diary with the illustration of a girl on front who had huge dark eyes and a giant wild mane of hair formed out of wispy lines and gorgeous floating neon flowers. I was enamored with the electric colors and the mystique of knowing it came from an

era I hadn't lived in," Missy says of her early exposure to the big-eyed girl, Japanese kitsch look that would later inspire both her work and her extraordinary collection of vintage cute.

As for the sweets theme and the irresistibly playful appearance of confections that run through much of her photography, Missy blames her relentless viewing, when she was little, of a short Disney cartoon from 1935 called *The Cookie Carnival*. "Brightly colored candy just courts my heart," she says. "The exhilaration one feels at the sight of candy seems a universal thing, really, but for some—like me—it's something I've always found myself fervently drawn to."

Missy's love of cheery candy colors and treats-themed imagery has also spilled over into her successful doll line. Not much of a sewer, she teamed up with her mom, Donna Kost, to help bring the first Boopsie Daisy doll to life in 2008. Missy designs the dolls, her mom does the sewing, and Missy paints the faces before the dolls are scented with sweet smells like cotton candy, jelly bean, and butter cookie. "The goal is to create a doll that looks good enough to eat—so she should smell edible, too," Missy says. "In fact, one girl in Tokyo confessed to me that the temptation once became too great for her and she took a bite of her Boopsie doll head."

Missy's dolls have developed such a fervent cult following that they sell out within seconds at her online Etsy shop (*etsy.com/shop/boopsie daisy*), and she continues to add to her body of photography work as well. She's always on the hunt for cute foodstuffs to incorporate into her photographs. Just be warned if you're ever invited over to her place for a meal. "[My family] loves to recount the number of times I have interrupted breakfast or a barbeque to whip out my camera and stuff a doll head inside a chicken breast or pour a bottle of sauce over a toy."

Etsy: etsy.com/shop/boopsiedaisy
Flickr: flickr.com/photos/boopsiedaisy/
Blog: boopsiedaisy.blogspot.ca/

A batch of Easter dolls made by Missy Munday in 2009. Photo: Missy Munday

Hello, Cutie!

Say Cheese!

Rosanna Mackney

Photo: Tofu Cute

Say "food with a face" to any cute hunter, and the big smile you're sure to elicit has absolutely nothing to do with vegetarianism or the politics of eating animals. Rather, it means plush donuts with grins and edamame soybean pod key chains that, with just a quick squeeze, reveal a happy-faced, green pop-up bean. Welcome to the world of Tofu Cute, an online retailer based in the UK that specializes in Japanese snacks and super-cute novelties.

One of Tofu Cute's founders, Rosanna Mackney, has always been a fan of cute things, from collectable stickers to kitschy Furby toys. In fact, it was the Furby that introduced Rosanna and her business partner to online selling in the first place. When they were studying at university, the pair began collecting and refurbishing (no pun intended) the electronic toys, then selling them on the Internet. The business was a success and soon they started carrying new toys, though it wasn't the big American brand names that got their customers' attention. "We found that there

was so much competition from Toys "R" Us or Walmart—all the big stores that are so price-driven—that [the toys that sold] the best were the rarer, more gadgety Japanese toys."

The demand in the UK for unique Japanese products was apparent, and after identifying the food-with-faces niche, Tofu Cute went live in 2010. "The food with faces theme occurred to us, and we thought we could base a brand around it, so every time we would see a product that featured food with faces, we'd jump on it," says Rosanna.

The response was immediate, with many customers returning weekly to the Tofu Cute site to place orders for rare, limited-edition boxes of the Japanese snack sticks known as Pocky and food-with-a-face novelties such as stuffies and stationery. And while there's an unmistakable market for such products, not everyone gets it. "We're so used to it—we're surrounded by it every day," says Rosanna, noting that not everyone who visits *tofucute. com* can always identify just what the food is supposed to be. "Looking at a plush wasabi with a face, we'll say, 'Oh, that's wasabi.' Other people will point to the product and ask, 'What on earth is that?' To us it seems so normal now."

Tofu Cute's best-seller, the Endless Edamame Popping Soybean Pod. Photo: Tofu Cute

tofucute.com
Twitter: @tofu_cute
Facebook: facebook.com/tofucute
Flickr: flickr.com/tofu_cute

A selection of Tofu Cute's products. Photo: Tofu Cute

Hello, Cutie!

Objects of Desire

I don't collect for the sake of collecting. I'm not a person who keeps items in their original boxes, displayed in specially designed cabinets. I don't have a long list of things I collect—that list grows and shrinks, morphing over time, the only true constants being vintage clothes, textiles, and fashion magazines, books about pop culture and design and, of course, cute objects: mostly dolls, toys, and mid-century made-in-Japan curios. All of these things I've collected since my mid-teens, but the collecting bug bit me much earlier.

I've always been a collector of the kitsch and the cute, long before I knew that many of my beloved pieces are considered by some as tacky and tasteless. I've been accused more than once of being obsessive about my collections, but I prefer to think it's all very ordered and, above all, focused.

The earliest memory I have of the collecting impulse was my childhood appetite for stuffed animals—and then for more stuffed animals. I must have been quite young when it started, maybe five. I arranged them carefully on my bed every day and gave them all names, albeit not always particularly original ones. There was Teddy Bear Two, a gift from my grandmother, and Lindy, a huge plush lioness stretched out in repose. Then there was a puppet called Honey Bear that my uncle sent while he was traveling in Switzerland, and later Pandy, the toy panda bear brought back from a trip to China by my father. I made stuffed animals, too, when I learned to sew.

Looking around my daughter's bedroom, I get a strange sense of deja-vu. They're not neatly arranged, but her bed is piled with stuffies. There are no less than four storage bins tucked away in the corner as well, filled with her collections of Care Bears, Webkinz, and Li'l Peepers. She can't bear to give any of them up, and a couple of times a year, every one of

Flocked lamb, 1950s

Hello, Cutie!

her hundreds of stuffies are freed and brought out for a giant play session before returning to storage.

The appeal of stuffed toys is obvious: they're soft and cuddly and usually cute. I imagine that they've been staple playthings for centuries, so I'm surprised to discover that commercially made stuffies didn't come onto the market until the late nineteenth century, when the German toy company Steiff introduced a small, densely stuffed elephant made of furry fabric. It was designed for use as a pincushion, but found unexpected demand as a children's toy. Steiff animals didn't flop around like homemade rag dolls and were crafted to resemble real animals rather than the anthropomorphized versions with exaggerated features that are the hallmark of many contemporary stuffed toys.

Vintage Steiff animals, often made of mohair material, can fetch thousands of dollars, even in threadbare condition. I log onto eBay and find that a "Mr. Wilfred Pickles" Steiff bear from 1906 recently sold for over $7,000. This alleviates any guilt I have been harboring since purchasing a Steiff poodle for my daughter at the famed Obletter's toyshop in Munich for around sixty-five dollars. A bit of research tells me that Steiffs of any era hold their value well, but if you find a turn-of-the-century Steiff teddy bear, you've hit the jackpot.

I dig a little deeper into the origins of the stuffie and find that exactly who deserves the bragging rights for selling the world's first commercial teddy bear is a contentious issue. American Morris Michtom—a Russian immigrant who went on to found the Ideal Novelty and Toy Company—is often credited, along with his wife Rose, as the source of the very first teddy bear. The story goes like this: in November 1902, US President Theodore Roosevelt was on a hunting expedition when his party encountered a black bear. The men wrangled the bear and tied it to a tree, but the President would not allow anyone to kill the animal. The press went wild for the story, and inspired by a political cartoon in *The Washington Post* depicting Roosevelt refusing to let the bear be shot, Rose made a couple of stuffed bears. Morris put them on display in the window of his Brooklyn novelty shop and soon they couldn't produce the toys—called "Teddy's Bear"—fast enough.

But that same year, over in Germany, Margarete Steiff's nephew, Richard, designed a jointed bear called "Bear 55 PB." The toy caused a big stir at the Leipzig Toy Fair in 1903, and was picked up by an American businessman who bought and imported 3,000 of the bears. Like the Michtoms' bear, the Steiff toys were an instant hit, though which really came first remains a matter for nit-picking historians.

Plastic teddy bear piggy bank, Canada, 1970s, ©Regal Toy

Hello, Cutie!

One thing that is not in dispute, however, is that the name "teddy bear" was derived from the Michtoms and their Teddy Roosevelt tribute, and by 1906, even the Steiff bears were sold as "teddy bears."

Some people collect teddy bears. I collect big-eyed Japanese dolls and old-fashioned magazines. My daughter has reams of Pokémon cards and stuffies. Everyone seems to collect something, and I can't help but wonder why. What drives this urge to amass so many of such specific things? There is, of course, no one answer to this; the desire to keep a connection to the past is one of the most common theories, but isn't the only motive for collecting. I take a few moments and stare blankly at my computer screen. If I want answers, I'm probably going to have to wade through a whole lot of academic jargon and psychology talk to get them.

Only one book and a few magazine articles in, and I realize that the psychologists are divided on the subject of collecting. Some say it's a natural stage of childhood, often driven by innocent curiosity and the subconscious desire for control. Collecting can trigger harmless escapism, whether it's stuffed animals or seashells—or anything in between—that captures our interest. Some of these same impulses fuel the collecting bug of adults, one camp of psychologists believe, but unless the habit crosses the line from hobby to hoarding,

Vinyl toy kitten, 1950s

collecting is not generally seen as a sinister or disruptive force in our lives.

Our motives for collecting range from aesthetic preferences and tastes to a desire for a showcase to display our individualism, to a need for completion or "allness" in the case of those who work (and spend) tirelessly to complete a particular collection. But not everyone shares these considerate views of collecting and collectors, something I notice almost immediately upon cracking the spine of Werner Muensterberger's book, *Collecting: An Unruly Passion: Psychological Perspectives*.

The psychoanalyst and psychiatry professor—who passed away in 2011—studied

Hand-painted ceramic piggy bank, 1960s

Hello, Cutie!

collectors for decades, drawing on experience and case studies from his personal practice as well as data and anecdotes relating to history and anthropology. This is all very impressive, I think, and am keen to read all about these psychological perspectives. But soon I am not.

Muensterberger holds a very dim—even dark—view of collectors. They are damaged souls—all of them. They've suffered childhood trauma and seek solace in objects. They anthropomorphize mere things, assign emotion to them, and have difficulty relating to actual humans. If he's to be believed, collecting is a form of anxiety relief, a way to ward off depression and deal with abandonment issues. In his words: "there is evidence of these traits in all dedicated collectors." He goes on to say that collecting can also be a manifestation of narcissism, providing an ego boost to collectors who derive a sense of uniqueness and power from possessing items they falsely believe bring them power when, in fact, this behavior is simply masking deep-seeded insecurity. It's not a pretty picture, and after nearly 300 pages, I'm not sure whether I'm angry or ashamed, and end up feeling a bit of both.

I know a lot of collectors. I am a collector and so is my daughter. Yes, everyone has quirks and baggage, but even though I'm not a psychologist, it's hard for me to believe that all of the smart, delightful, and educated collectors I've met over the years are actually self-loathing egoists who have lost touch with reality.

Muensterberger's low view of collectors is annoying, but isn't likely to quell any of our passion. He's made me think, though, that maybe there are nuggets of truth in his work, even if I'm not prepared to adopt his opinions in full. Maybe collecting can be a temporary escape from reality, but is that really so bad? Reality is not the best place to be for many people in these times, especially from a socio-economic perspective. And the emphasis on connecting to the past that so many of Muensterberger's contemporaries focus on in their hypotheses and research? That doesn't seem so bad either. There's something wistful, if not romantic, about being motivated by times past (not to mention that this paints a much more palatable image of the collector), and it's something many cute collectors can relate to.

Nostalgia certainly plays some role in many of our collecting habits, and the kind of cute stuff being collected by a lot of people is often linked to our childhoods, now more than ever. I remember as a teenager groaning whenever a commercial for one of those "oldies" record collections came on. *Yuck*, I thought. *Who would want to listen to anything that sounded like* that? It was the 1980s. Greed was good, and the shinier and newer, the better.

But slowly, a shift in North American youth subculture took place, and "vintage" emerged

Inflatable cat, Hong Kong, 1970s

Hello, Cutie!

as vogue. Vintage was different than antique. To us, antique meant old. Vintage was fashion and represented a specific aesthetic. Whether it was clothing or *tchotchke* kitsch, mixing mid-century items into our lives was chic. Our parents didn't understand why we would haunt thrift shops and junk sales, why we would want to wear someone else's old clothes, when they were happy to buy us new ones. Clothing was the portal most people took into vintage-world, but like many collectors, I soon found my collections diversifying. I traveled regularly to small towns with like-minded friends in search of the next treasure. We relished the thrill of the hunt and loved our finds even better. We outfitted our first apartments in loudly colored '60s furniture and placed cutesy toys and knick-knacks on every surface. Perhaps we did buy into a kind of nostalgia. It wasn't for our own youth, but that of some imaginary retro friend.

Today, there is no stigma attached to thrift stores, and buying vintage is more popular than ever thanks to the boom of second-hand shopping online. Almost everything possible has been labeled "collectible," whether it actually commands—or has the potential in the future to command—any real monetary value or not. And unlike my teenage experience collecting vintage items that were manufactured long before I was born, a more personal and contemporary interpretation of nostalgia has emerged as the number of re-collectors swells.

Sentimental and eager to capture the spirit of their childhood collecting experience, re-collectors actively seek and purchase the same items they had as kids, the ones that were worn out, given away, sold, or lost in a move. This trend reminds me of a book I read a while back called *Rejuvenile: Kickball, Cartoons, Cupcakes, and the Reinvention of the American Grown-up*, about adults who engage in play and activities typically associated with childhood, whether that means skateboarding to work or visiting Disneyland sans kids. These "rejuveniles" that author Christopher Noxon describes are also fans of side-by-side play with their own children, and re-reading his book I find all sorts of parallels with my own life and relationship with my daughter, so I send him a note, figuring he may have an opinion on re-collecting.

It turns out that Christopher, an American journalist based in Los Angeles, lived in Montreal during the same period I was there in the early 1990s, and we end up chatting a bit about Canadian politics and the Quebec separatist movement that resulted in social and economic trouble during that time. I also tell him about a game I used to play with a friend there that we called "Metro Stops We've Never Been To." If we were bored, we'd pick a stop on the Montreal subway map, go there, and explore the neighborhood. Christopher likes this idea,

Plush mouse, 1960s

which is no surprise considering how playful it is. The game has a touch of the rejuvenile spirit, perhaps foreshadowing my foray later in life into serious kid stuff.

"The pursuit of childhood toys is a gateway drug into the world of rejuveniles," says Christopher, explaining that the memories such toys evoke can result in an emotional reawakening, prompting feelings in adults that they haven't experienced in a long time. He also believes that just as re-collectors—and rejuveniles in general—find inspiration inside themselves to collect toys or play like kids, outside stressors like economic and social instability influence the phenomenon as well. "Many people go back to the last frame of mind when they felt safe," he says. This makes perfect sense to me and echoes the theories about why cute culture as a whole is a growing, grown-up concern.

Not everyone is a dedicated rejuvenile or on a quest to reclaim their childhood toys, but thanks to the recent spate of brand relaunches, they may not have to be to capture a version of their good old days. Everything old seems to be new again in toyland with re-launches of '80s toys like Strawberry Shortcake, My Little Pony, Polly Pocket, Pound Puppies, Cabbage Patch Kids, and Littlest Pet Shop, to name but a few. It's hard to determine whether the marketing executives working behind the scenes are taking advantage of an existing market for older brands or if they're creating one. Whatever the case, it's working, and one of the unique side effects of the re-launch trend is multi-generational collecting, particularly among moms and their girls.

Moms fondly remember the toys from their own childhood, so it makes perfect sense that they'd buy the revamped version for their daughters (and maybe for themselves, too). Moms get in touch with their memories, and the girls create new ones, and in twenty years they can do it all over again with the grandkids. It's all pretty genius when you think about it—and awfully hard to resist.

In this regard, the traditional mother-daughter divide has shrunk. It's no longer considered especially strange or silly for grown-ups to buy or collect toys. As kids of the consumerist 1970s, '80s, and '90s, many of our best memories are attached to objects, so it's perfectly easy to understand how a version of a cute plastic pony we once had can become a source of bonding with our own children.

But as well intentioned as we may be in taking our kids for a trip down toy-memory lane, it doesn't always work, as I discovered when I bought my daughter a Cabbage Patch Kid. It was 2003 and shortly before Christmas. I was in New York and the giant Toys "R" Us in Times Square was selling the newly relaunched dolls. They hadn't been rolled out to the masses yet, so I saw this as a great opportunity to pick one up for my daughter.

The doll's name was Octavia and reminded me of my own Cabbage Patch Kid, Laura, who I fought the crowds to get in 1983. I was thirteen—a bit old for baby dolls—and I didn't really like them that much. My mother remembers that I thought Cabbage Patch Kids were weird, so naturally I had to have one. I also had to have one for another reason. My entrepreneurial teenage brain had noticed that there were no clothes for the dolls, and indeed, the demand for dolls was so great that Coleco, the company that produced them, was putting most of its efforts into manufacturing as many of the dolls as possible before Christmas.

I could sew and make up basic patterns, and once I had my doll, I got straight to work, spending my weekends and after-school hours whipping up little lace-trimmed dresses, pajamas, shirts, and pants. I placed an ad in the community newsletter and on the notice board in the entrance of the local grocery store, and within days, mothers were calling me, anxious to get their hands on some extra clothes for their child's doll. I would lay everything out neatly on the dining room table and more often than not, my customers would buy up the whole lot, and I'd have to start over again, making more clothes from cotton remnants I bought for nearly nothing at the local fabric store. My parents found this all quite hilarious, most notably because I didn't initially tell them my plans; they found out when frazzled ladies, struck with Cabbage Patch fever, started turning up at the front door.

Considering my experience, I think it's completely reasonable that I have always had a soft spot for Cabbage Patch Kids, but soft spot or not, my daughter wanted nothing to do with Octavia, going as far as to throw her violently face-down on the floor whenever I'd try to encourage some Cabbage Patch play time. Even when she warmed to dolls, at around age eight or nine, Octavia remained shunned, stuffed into a corner, a winter-weight duvet on top of her.

Cabbage Patch Kids were the first significant cute craze I remember, but definitely not

Little Miss Lucky & Mr. Funny PVC figurines, Taiwan, 1991, ©Hargreaves LLC

Hello, Cutie!

the last. Three of the most significant fads in the past two decades have been Tickle Me Elmo, Tamagotchi, and Furby. What makes kids and adults alike go mad for a particular toy? Perhaps a closer look at the successes will give me some clues.

Tickle Me Elmo kicked off a rapid succession of cute crazes that took place in the latter part of the 1990s. A furry red creature of indeterminable species, Elmo was—and still is—a character on the children's television show *Sesame Street*. While *Sesame Street* has long been a popular program, the success of the squeeze-my-tummy-and-make-me-giggle Tickle Me Elmo was not entirely related to the show.

Sure, there were the parents who pushed and shoved—and in one case in Canada, maimed a Walmart employee who was trying to get a new shipment of Elmos on the shelves—in an effort to buy their pre-schoolers a giggly plush version of their favorite television character, but what was surprising is that about twenty-one percent of the one million Elmos sold during that heady holiday season in 1996 were to teenagers.

These kids weren't likely big *Sesame Street* viewers any longer, but there's a good chance they may have caught sight of the toy in action on one of the popular talk shows of the time like *Regis & Kathie Lee* or the *Rosie O'Donnell Show*. Tickle Me Elmo became a staple on the talk-show circuit that fall, with celebrities squeezing his little belly to make him laugh. No traditional advertising could possibly have had the impact Elmo's television appearances did, and suddenly toy company Tyco couldn't manufacture them fast enough.

People were wild about Elmo—quite literally, in fact. Predicting a supply shortage, some unscrupulous sellers hoarded whatever dolls they could get their hands on, only to sell them, as the clock to Christmas ticked down, to desperate parents at grossly inflated prices. The doll—which retailed for around thirty dollars—was being sold for over $1,000, sometimes as much as $1,500. The only thing more insane than the Tickle Me Elmo craze itself were the people who actually paid such ridiculous prices for one.

As Elmo-mania was sweeping across North America, another cute craze was enthralling kids, teens, and adults half a world away. In late 2006, Tokyo toy company Bandai unleashed the Tamagotchi into the Japanese market. In just four months, over 1.5 million units were sold, and by spring word had started to filter into the Western press about these strange electronic-egg-watch-creature things. I don't know if any of us knew what to make of these reports. *Only in Japan*, I remember thinking. But, boy was I wrong.

Not all Japanese trends make it big in the West, but Tamagotchi sure did. Having only

Care Bears' Grumpy Bear, China, 2002, ©American Greetings Corporation, Inc.

Hello, Cutie!

recently recovered from Tickle Me Elmo overload, Tamagotchi swept in; soon, everywhere we went, we heard that little "pip" sound the Creature inside the egg made when it was happy.

If you've never come face-to-face with a Tamagotchi, let me explain: oval-shaped and the size of an average key ring, Tamagotchi is a very small, very simple electronic game designed originally for children. It was one of the first "virtual pet" simulations. At first, there's just an egg on the tiny screen, but once you set the clock, it will hatch within minutes. Now the fun begins. You are responsible for your new pet, so you have to feed it, play with it, and give it plenty of attention. You also are required to discipline your pet and clean up after it pees or poos. Sound like a lot of work? It is. Pets, virtual or otherwise, are demanding.

The commitment necessary to care for a Tamagotichi didn't stop millions of consumers worldwide from "adopting" one. From Japan, the craze spread to Britain, finally landing in North America in May 1997 with a price tag of between twenty-five to thirty dollars each. With so much international press hype, the gotta-get-it-first shoppers clamored to get one, followed by the masses, and within two years of its introduction, over 20 million pets had been sold.

But not everyone jumped on the Tamagotchi bandwagon. The toys were distracting, with their beeping and constant demand for attention. They were the bane of many a teacher's existence in their heyday, and schools began to ban students from bringing their pets to class; some wouldn't even allow them on school grounds. The high-maintenance electronic creatures suffered from the lack of attention. Innumerable pets died. Tears were shed and parents begged to buy another.

There were later editions of the toy designed with pets that were somewhat less demanding, but the principle remained the same. Like all cute crazes, the good times eventually come to an end, and by the end of 1998, sales had tapered dramatically. In 2004 there was an attempt to revive the brand with the Tamagotchi Plus, and new Tamagotchi-themed video games have been released consistently since 2005. (I have to admit that my daughter and I bought a copy of *Tamagotchi: Party On!* for Wii because we thought the characters on the display box were so cute.) Tamagotchi has morphed into a brand rather than just a toy. The name has not disappeared from store shelves or from our cute consciousness, as most fads do.

Hot on the heels of Tickle Me Elmo and Tamagotchi was the much-loved—and much-loathed—talking robot toy Furby. Introduced in 1998, Furby completed an unprecedented three-year run of cute crazes. While there are always must-have toys each year, a full-blown

My Little Pony Star Catcher pegasus pony, China, 2007, ©Hasbro

Hello, Cutie!

craze is rare; three years in a row is even more unusual.

Furby itself was unusual, with its big eyes and ears, beak, thick hind legs, and tuft of hair. Just what kind of animal Furby was wasn't the question everyone was asking: it was *Where can I get one?* Or, in the case of Furby-haters, *Will you please get that thing away from me?* The polarizing creature was creepy to some, cute to others. But the anti-Furby camp couldn't stop 40 million of the things flying off shelves in its first two years of production.

Furbies, as anyone who has ever met one knows, speak Furbish, a language only they understand. But over time, the toys start to speak English. They also move around and open and close their eyes and beaks, and—most strangely—communicate with other Furbies in Furbish. More sophisticated Emoto-Tronic Furbies were released in 2005 and 2006 that could communicate better with their human owners and obey simple commands thanks to built-in voice-recognition software.

The attempt at a Furby comeback fizzled, though some hackers and circuit benders have been seeking out original Furbies for years, taking them apart and modifying their electronic innards or replacing their circuit boards in order to make the toys say specific things and make certain sounds. There are hundreds of online tutorials to walk a newbie through the process step-by-step, so if you've got an old Furby kicking around collecting dust, it's good to know that you have options.

Tickle Me Elmo, Tamagotchi, Furby—all crazes, and all cute. Elmo and Furby had those big, yearning eyes and mischievous disposition; Tamagotchis were so small and helpless and needed our care. There's no magic formula in the toy business, but products with cute attributes and a novelty feature like giggling or talking or dying if you don't play with it are a good place to start for any aspiring toy designer.

Two true signs that you've got a bona fide cute craze on your hands are massive sales figures and physical altercations as shoppers fight to buy your item. More proof that people just can't get enough of the cute you're selling is the birth of fan message boards online where collectors can come together, share information and opinions, and post photographs of their prized collections.

Pick something cute—anything cute, as long as it is or has been popular at one time—and you're sure to find a message board out there to join. Collecting in isolation is not nearly as much fun as doing it as part of a group. You have people to talk to who are excited when you buy a new what-have-you. There are people to give you advice and whose personal collecting stories are fun to read. You can relate. They're your people. You may never meet any of them in person, but you know more about these faceless characters with funny names like *cutecollector1976* than you do about your neighbors—it's a community. And whatever you collect, there's probably a message board out there, tailor-made for you.

Message boards are funny things. They're a great source of information, but once you start reading through them you notice the same names popping up over and over, people seem to know each other well, and there are inside jokes and abbreviated language that can be hard at first to decipher. You may want to jump in and say something, but fear you may be shunned or laughed at for asking such a silly question. On the Dal and Blythe forums, I tentatively began to ask questions and was pleased with how helpful and friendly the

other collectors were. I don't post daily, but always check in and peek at what's being talked about.

When I log onto the Blythe doll message board *blythekingdom.com*, I find people looking for hair-styling advice for their dolls and others breathlessly excited about the arrival of a new one. As I scroll through the topics and comments, I start to think that perhaps the predominant theory among psychologist types—that we collect to keep a connection with the past—may be flawed in this information age. Perhaps the drive for some collectors of cute is to connect right now, with one another, and share our thoughts and stories, to be part of a community that's looking ahead, not back.

Hello, Cutie!

Pony Parade

ANNA COLLVER'S MY LITTLE PONY COLLECTION BRINGS CHILDHOOD BACK

Anna Collver

Photo: Anna Collver

Before Anna Collver sends me a photograph, I'm trying to picture what 3,000 My Little Ponies (or MLPs, as they're called by Pony fans) would look like. Each one is small, yes, but all together? I figure that 3,000 would fill a good part of an average bedroom—or at least a wall with special Pony-sized shelves.

I didn't have Ponies growing up, but my friends with younger sisters did, and more than two decades after their initial introduction in 1982, my daughter did too. She loved her Ponies. After her Care Bears phase, it was Ponies-Ponies-Ponies for two solid years. Then, like many kids, she moved on to the next obsession.

But more and more it's those items we loved as children that become the focus of our adult collections. Whether my daughter will return to Ponies one day remains to be seen, but there's no question that Anna Collver sure has—and in a big way. "I love MLP because it [represents] the happiness of my childhood,"

she says. "It was the highlight of my day to play MLP with my little sister and my friends. We loved to take them on adventures and trade them."

The original My Little Pony line was introduced by Hasbro the year Anna was born, and thanks to her older sister, who had Ponies of her own, the Portland, Oregon-based full-time university student and single mother of two doesn't remember a time without them. She collects new Ponies from the wildly popular Friendship Is Magic line, as well as vintage MLPs, her favorite being the unicorns that were produced in the '80s. She also prizes her uncommon foreign Ponies: "I have many French Ponies, an Italian Pony, and a Pony made in Thailand," she says. "The Thai Pony is probably the most unusual."

She's always on the lookout for a Baby Blossom, Ice Crystal, or Big Macintosh—three Ponies she'd love to add to her already impressive collection. She's scored rarities through online connections and happened upon unusual Ponies at local flea markets and thrift shops. But wherever and whenever she finds Ponies, Anna can't imagine life without her collection. "My Little Pony has been such a huge part of my life, and I cannot imagine a world without these brightly colored treasures," she says. "To me, MLP is worth more than anything."

Two of Anna Collver's most cherished Ponies, Blue Belle and Twilight. Photo: Anna Collver

Blog: annasponies.blogspot.com/
Flickr: flickr.com/photos/aquamaeanna/
collections/72157594587120722/

Anna Collver's My Little Pony collection. Photo: Anna Collver

Oh, Deer

VINTAGE DEALER SARA DOANE SPECIALIZES IN RETRO KITSCH

Sara Doane

Photo: Sara Doane

Tucked away in a small town in upstate New York, something very cute is happening. Knee-hugging elf toys with mischievous rubber heads sit next to plush Dakin Dream Pets and Japanese pose dolls. Toy squirrels mingle with squeaky toys amid miniature alpine cabins that double as music boxes. Cute hunters frequent Sara Doane's Etsy vintage shop (*etsy.com/shop/agent137*) for all of these things, but many shoppers come for the deer.

Since opening her shop in January 2011, Sara's store has become the go-to source for kitschy cute and it's her seemingly endless supply of deer themed items that sell best. She's always had a thing for cute ceramic and plastic does and fawns, many of which were manufactured in post-war Japan, and keeps a shelf of her favorites in her home. She comes from a family of collectors and follows in the footsteps of her mother and grandmother. It was from her own collections that the idea for opening a shop dedicated to kitschy-cute was spawned, and she was taken aback by the overwhelmingly positive—and immediate—response. Sales were made the same day she opened. Most fittingly, the first item she sold was a sweet, vintage plastic fawn. "Whenever I list a deer, it sells," she says.

To find her stock, Sara hits up garage and estate sales, scooping up anything with that big-eyed cute look. Her newfound profession is a far cry from the world she left behind after deciding a career in academia wasn't for her, but it's one she finds rewarding and hopes to continue pursuing. As for the deer, she's always on the lookout, and as the wave of interest in woodland animals grows among cute collectors, they're sure to keep on selling.

Etsy: etsy.com/shop/Agent137
Blog: agent137.blogspot.com/

Selections from
vintage dealer
Sara Doane's
deer collection.
Photos: Sara Doane

Hello, Cutie!

Making Nostalgia Modern

Alexandra Tyler

Leslie Dotson Van Every

Is it possible to make a new best friend on the phone? In an hour? What about two new best friends? I'm starting to think so after spending a bit of quality telephone time with Leslie Dotson Van Every and Alexandra Tyler of one of my favorite blogs, *modernkiddo.com*.

Better known to their readers as Dottie and Alix, the pair has been bringing fun into the daily lives of vintage hounds like me since 2010. Both moms and media professionals who live in the San Francisco Bay Area, Dottie and Alix met as members of a '60s retro go-go style dance troupe and one day got to talking about a website that Dottie wanted to start about vintage kids' clothing. The idea grew from there and Modern Kiddo was born. "It came from us wanting to bring the best of our past to our kids' present and finding a way to introduce them to the things that we loved, but also giving them room to explore and play and make some of these ideas their own," explains Alix.

The nostalgia of Modern Kiddo extends beyond fashion into toys, books, and décor. It's cute, but as Dottie is wont to stress, never cloying. It's also not

Photos: Alexandra Tyler

just for people with kids—anyone with a love of vintage will surely love a daily fix of color and cute.

"We call ourselves a nostalgia lifestyle blog," says Alix. "It's not solely for people who have children. I think it's for people who have these [childhood] memories. You just give them a nudge in the right direction. A lot of the shared experiences are what make the site so fun for us. People are constantly emailing us, or commenting with their own stories and forwarding us things. It's been really fun—and really rewarding that way."

The shopping links and tips Dottie and Alix put together are rewarding for the readers.

They scour Etsy and eBay for the cutest vintage buys and present them in weekly round-ups, celebrate fabulous illustrations found in vintage children's books and games, and share great DIY ideas for such things as repurposing vintage cotton sheets (you know, the ones with the Technicolor stripes or lively flowers).

The format has resonated strongly with readers. The site grew very quickly after its launch and helped fuel new interest in cute, vintage kids' fashion. When they started, there were lots of online sellers trying to focus on vintage children's clothing, but as Alix explains, unless you were an avid vintage person, it just wasn't something many people gave much thought to.

Thanks to Alix and Dottie, children's vintage is now on the radar, which is great in many ways, but can have its downside; as more people take an interest, many second-hand shops that were once teeming with cute kids' clothes are now picked-over—or prices have shot up. But all hope of finding that cute Cowichan sweater with a playing-puppies motif is not lost. "It's out there," Alix says. "You just have to look for it."

. . . .

Blog: modernkiddo.com
Twitter: @galexina
Instagram: @galexina

Modern Kiddo's Alexandra "Alix" Tyler's son Wolfie's retro style bedroom. Photos: Alexandra Tyler

Hello, Cutie!

Cute 'n' Creepy

IN CUTE CULTURE, ADORABLE AND SCARY AREN'T ALWAYS MUTUALLY EXCLUSIVE

*P*eteena was a grail doll for me. Not in the holy or religious sense, but as in the cute collectors' lexicon, an item that's at the top of our wish list, usually rare and often seriously expensive. But once in a while, that grail doll or toy or what-have-you comes up at a price far below market value and you happen to be in the right place at the right time and—huzzah!—it's all yours.

Such was the case with Peteena, the vintage poodle doll produced by Hasbro in 1966. It had been at least two years and maybe even three since I'd set my sights on owning this admittedly odd doll. There had been a few for sale on eBay, but I simply couldn't justify paying upwards of $150 for one. I'd nearly resigned myself to going through life Peteena-less when one was advertised on one of the doll forums I belong to for a fraction of the going rate. I snapped her up immediately, and after two weeks and a trans-Atlantic voyage from Germany, she was mine at last.

Not everyone was so enthused with my new doll, however. "It's creepy," my daughter said. She wouldn't even hold it. My fiancé didn't know what to make of her. "I wouldn't call it *cute*," he told me in the kindest way.

Okay, so she's not your everyday doll. Unlike any canines I know, she stands upright and has hands and feet, fingers and toes. She's got fancy eyelashes and wears makeup. She has long ears that are sort of dog-like, a curly tuft of off-white hair—fur?—on her head, and a fluffy tail on her bum. Peteena is a plastic fashion doll, and in her time had several mod fashion options to choose from. She's a bit like Barbie—if Barbie were a lady-poodle hybrid, that is. And she's cute. Or at least I think so. Because cute, as we have seen, is subjective. Just as one woman finds a certain man wildly attractive and handsome, her best friend may very well not (in fact, she may find him wildly unattractive and homely). The same goes for cute. What's curious is that it's the word creepy

Peteena doll, Japan,1966, ©Hasbro

Hello, Cutie!

that comes up in describing the antithesis of cute most frequently.

I do a bit of reading and discover that this is not unusual. Remember all of those psychological theories as to why we find things cute? The big eyes and heads, the round faces and expressions of helplessness that pull at our heartstrings? Well, it's those very same attributes that can make us think of something as morbid or ugly. Think of horror movie monsters' disproportioned faces and figures, the crazy, bulging eyes. Now think of a cute dolly, stuffed animal, or figurine like the ones I've discussed, and recall their oversized heads and giant eyes. Cute or creepy?

A very fine line separates the cute from the creepy, the attractive from the grotesque, empathy from revulsion. Throw a Peteena into the conversation and you're bound to elicit myriad opinions, running the gamut from extremely adorable to extremely upsetting. It's all a matter of taste, which depends to some extent on an individual's personal tolerance for kitsch. Like creepy and cute, kitsch is a word bandied about by many collectors on a near-daily basis. But what does it really mean to say that something is kitsch?

In nineteenth-century Germany, kitsch was used to describe art that was popular and cheap. In twentieth-century North America, the definition hadn't really changed. Kitsch held steady as a derogatory term in arts and

Gorgeous Creatures' Princess Pig, Philippines, 1979, ©Mattel

culture circles. But by the early twenty-first century, an appreciation of kitsch began to evolve and infiltrate the mainstream, and more often than not it's tied to images or items that are cute—or creepy.

Creepy-cute is what I like to call those polarizing things like Peteena, which really do divide people into two distinct camps. Tacky and tasteless, garish and gaudy are all words that come up when I start discussing kitsch with my cute-collecting friends. None of these characterizations are positive, but somehow when they add up to kitsch, they are—at least to us. We know that Peteena and her ilk are all

Gloomy Bear, China, 2003, ©Mori Chack

Hello, Cutie!

of those things: tacky, tasteless, garish, gaudy, but we love them still, maybe even because of.

We seek out the kitsch and are drawn to things that hover in the unresolved area between creepy and cute. I have about fifty plastic Halloween masks that I use in my photography work. Most are of animals, and for a small fee my increasingly market-savvy daughter will pose in them for me. I've been shooting this series on and off for five years, and the two words my buyers use most are cute and creepy. When I look at the work I see both sides: they're creepy-cute, I think, and part of a burgeoning aesthetic preference among collectors of everything from fine art to vintage toys.

Like kitsch, creepy is not a dirty word among the cute collectors I know, and the creepy-cute aesthetic is absolutely embraced—just ask Julia Chibatar, founder of the Etsy team Spooky Cute. A crafter who specializes in year-round Halloween items—especially those with a bat theme—Julia has a personal affection for mixing the cute with the creepy and suspected there might be others out there who felt the same. The Spooky Cute team, which serves as a hub for Etsy sellers with similar interests, launched in February 2012 and took off immediately. "I can't believe how fast people are joining this team," Julia says, speaking to me from her home in Kissimmee, Florida. It's clear that both sellers and buyers have a hankering for creepy-cute, whether it's handmade, vintage, or a current import from Japan.

One of my favorite examples of creepy-cute is Gloomy Bear, created by Japanese graphic designer, Mori Chack. Gloomy the bear is cute and cuddly, but he is still a bear and will attack you if he gets the chance. Gloomy is owned by a boy called Pitty, and as you can imagine, things do not go well for the pair. This is the official story:

"Gloomy Bear, an abandoned little bear, is rescued by Pitty (the little boy). At first, he is cute and cuddly, but becomes more wild as he grows up. Since bears do not become attached to people like dogs by nature, Gloomy attacks Pitty even though he is the owner. So Gloomy has blood on him from biting and/or scratching Pitty."

It's hardly the heart-warming story of Hello Kitty living in suburban London and weighing three apples. But the juxtaposition of the cute and the creepy has made Gloomy Bear an international success. You can buy Gloomy stuffed animals (with or without bloodied claws and mouth), stationery, and lunch boxes. My first Gloomy purchase was a keychain with a jointed bear and tiny Pitty dangling from it, his expression typically pained.

Gloomy Bear may be well known in creepy-cute circles and among collectors of Japanese novelties, but the most famous of all contemporary creepy-cute brands has got to be the Uglydoll. Launched in 2001 by illustrator

Roly-poly clown, Canada, 1970s, ©Regal Canada

Hello, Cutie!

David Horvath and his now-wife, Sun-Min Kim, the stuffed, handmade toys have simple body shapes and eyes that are simply two widely spaced circles with a black dot in the center of each. They're cartoonish, like a child's drawing of a not-so-scary monster—more *South Park* than fancy Hollywood CGI.

I read up on the history of Uglydoll, and its story is decidedly more cute than creepy. The genesis of the dolls came when Sun-Min Kim moved back to her native Korea to be with her family. David Horvath, who was her boyfriend at the time, wrote letters to her and drew pictures on them of a funny little creature with two small horns atop his head, the aforementioned circle-and-dot eyes, and a long straight line for a mouth, with a single fang at either end. Kim surprised her beau by making a stuffed toy of the Creature as a gift. That creature became Wage, the first Uglydoll, and a creepy-cute icon was born.

The toys were first sold in New York at Giant Robot, and from there an ardent fan-base grew. Rather than being a typically short-lived fad, the Uglydoll empire has continued to grow and gain followers. There are now all kinds of Uglydoll merchandise, including T-shirts, tote bags, and umbrellas, and a feature film is set for release in 2013. I wonder about what is so appealing about Uglydoll that its consumer base has kept growing while other not-so-creepy-cute brands fall out of favor after a single season.

Uglydolls may have been the biggest hit of the last ten years, but it's not like creepy-cute is a new thing. As a matter of fact, it's a very, very old thing. Clowns are the oldest of the creepy-cute species, and evidence of their existence dates all the way back to ancient Egypt. In those days, before the term "clown" was coined, fools were employed to entertain the powerful and wealthy. Cruelly, most of these "fools" were, in fact, people with handicaps.

The court jester of the late Middle Ages was the first step toward the clowns we know today. Early jesters were known for their whimsical costumes, silly dances, and funny jokes. Jesters and fools were treated with derision by the nobility whom they served (think of Shakespeare's Fool in *King Lear*) and were regularly insulted and even assaulted. But as the jester became the clown, these characters evolved a wittiness to balance their traditional buffoonery. But it is the decidedly more low-brow circus clown that we most often think of when the word is mentioned. The first circus clowns appeared in late eighteenth-century England, later migrating across the Atlantic to the United States, where the modern clown found its true footing.

Clown merchandise was largely a product of the 1950s, and we have the television birthday clown to blame for that. For decades, children's programs had a resident clown who would often sing, dance, and read out the names of kids with birthdays that day or week who had written to the show in hopes of hearing their name read aloud on television.

When I was growing up, it was Bimbo, the unfortunately named Birthday Clown on the Canadian noon-time classic the *Uncle Bobby Show*, that I remember best. I loved watching Uncle Bobby and Bimbo, the giant two-dimensional painted clown and his family of crocheted clowns that would fall from the ceiling and "fly" across the stage using clearly visible wire. But now, looking at old clips on YouTube, the whole thing seems much more creepy than cute.

For some, clowns—live or inanimate—go beyond creepy. Fear of clowns is well-documented and even has a name: coulrophobia, though the term is a product of pseudo-science, rather than one that was coined by psychologists, and is accepted among some mental health professionals. I learn that it is, in fact, the third most common phobia in Britain while listening to an NPR broadcast about John Lawson's Circus, a company that offers therapy to coulrophobics before their performances in the UK.

Personally, I have no issues with clowns. Real, live performing clowns I could take or leave, but give me a hot-pink plastic, blow-mold roly-poly clown made in Japan circa the 1970s, and I'm happy. I have three such clowns lined up on my bookshelves, arranged with three Kewpie doll friends. With their big bellies and smiley faces, I can't understand how they could be considered anything but cute.

The first toy clown I owned as an adult was a prop from a film I worked on, which wasn't used by the set decorators. I brought him to the production office where he became our mascot, much to the chagrin of the film's location manager. Daryl was petrified of clowns, and it wasn't long before Mr. Clown, as I had named him, became his nemesis. We played silly jokes such as hiding Mr. Clown in Daryl's desk or stuffing him into his bag or his car. There was something almost unbelievable about a grown man being so scared of such an innocent—and in my opinion, cute—toy clown. Eventually, we stopped the shenanigans after Daryl took his fist to Mr. Clown, indenting the hard plastic face.

At the end of filming, I claimed Mr. Clown as my own and then found two matching clowns in quick succession. My mother thought it was amusing that I would collect three of the same clown toys I had and played with as a baby. *What?* I had no idea that I had a Mr. Clown as a child. But maybe buried somewhere deep in my subconscious there was a memory of this friendly clown. Maybe Daryl had one too, as a kid, but hated it.

Clowns are quintessentially creepy-cute, inspiring both detractors, like Daryl, and ardent fans. I think it's safe to say that Crystal Faith Scott is ensconced firmly in the fan camp. Crystal wrote the script for and stars in the indie film *Girl Clown*, about a woman who takes up work as a birthday-party clown to help overcome her shyness. The plot isn't a huge leap for Crystal, an actor in New York City who works as a professional birthday party clown between jobs. Dressed in her super-cute red-and-white clown costume, she's found that most people have a clown-positive attitude towards her. "When I go to my gigs, I usually walk or take the subway. And I'm always dressed in my clown costume," she says. "When I first started doing this, I noticed something interesting—people would always smile at me. Some would wave and even shout 'hello!' from across the street. They would inevitably stop and ask me questions: 'How did you become a clown?' 'That must be a fun job!' 'Did you make your own costume?'" That friendly reception sometimes gets a bit *too* friendly, if not weird. "The funniest is when I get asked out on a date when I'm in clown costume. I'm always thinking, wait—are you actually hitting on a *clown*?"

Crystal may not fit the image of a creepy clown, a stereotype she's keen to dispel, preferring to embrace the lighter, cuter side of clowning. "Before they've actually seen or met me, people say that they don't like clowns," she says. "A lot of people have an 'idea' in their mind of what a clown is. Usually that is a big tall guy covered in white-face paint with a scary wig."

Crystal Scott in *Girl Clown: The Film*.
Photo: Michael Canterino

Crystal Scott doesn't look scary at all, whether she's in full clown regalia or not. I don't think the smiley-faced red toy piano or the pair of ceramic dogs with fake-fur hair-dos on the shelf above my desk are menacing either. But that's just me. While clowns may encourage heated creepy-cute debate, it's anthropomorphism that really gets cute collectors talking.

It's easy and typical of us to assign human attributes to objects and animals, to planets and even businesses. Anthropomorphism can be subtle or overt, and in relation to creepy-cute, it's almost always obvious.

Moving eye clock, Japan, 1960s, ©Mi-Ken

Hello, Cutie!

You can put a face on anything—literally. I have a vintage wind-up apple-shaped piggy bank with mischievous eyes and a strange little "worm" that pops out of its mouth to grab the coin placed on the designated spot and then disappear into the innards of the bank with it. The worm also has a face. I have a vintage red-and-white plastic cup with a built-in straw and a clown face with googly eyes from the American soft-serve ice cream chain Tastee Freez. All over my home there are faces on things that shouldn't have faces at all.

Advertisers learned early in the twentieth century that anthropomorphizing anything could help distinguish their brands and cultivate a friendly and cute image simply by putting a face on it—whether it was a pair of smiling, pineapple-shaped salt-and-pepper shakers, an original Mr. Potato Head, or anything in between. Food companies and suppliers of kitchen wares were some of the first to jump on the anthropomorphism bandwagon in the first half of the twentieth century. They made dish towels embroidered with dancing plates and spoons and dinner settings of red ceramic apple-theme dishes with the sweetest expressions. It was possible to have your kitchen kitted out entirely with items bearing friendly faces. And the anthropomorphism didn't end there; consumers were introduced to the Chiquita Banana and Planter's Mr. Peanut, two of the best-known advertising characters

of all time and prime examples of creepy-cute aesthetic.

Food company advertising characters have come and gone (remember King Salad? Lily Lemon? Red Magic the Aristocrat Tomato?), but Mr. Peanut has endured for nearly 100 years. The hoity-toity yellow peanut wears a top hat and white gloves, and sports a monocle in one eye; he carries a cane and has short white booties on his feet. He's a bit of a dandy, a man about town, an *Esquire*-reading gentleman with an eye for the ladies—at least that's how I've always pictured him.

That I've imagined the extra-curricular activities of a fictional peanut with a face at all is strange when I really think about it. That slapping a face on a peanut and donning it with fashion accessories is enough for me to assign the character a full-blown persona and assume his penchant for witty repartee is more than weird, especially considering that Mr. Peanut didn't utter a single word until 2010 when actor Robert Downey Jr, supplied his voice for an ad campaign. It's not that I find Mr. Peanut himself creepy—in fact, I think he's pretty cute, in an edible P.G. Wodehouse kind of way. What I do find creepy is how readily I fall for the whole anthropomorphism shtick. The same goes for the Miss Chiquita.

Created for Chiquita Bananas in 1944 by cartoonist Dik Browne and an instant success, she was a happy-go-lucky, dancing lady banana

Rubber-faced plush monkey doll, Canada, 1970s, ©Reliable Toy Co., Ltd.

Hello, Cutie!

in a Flamenco-style outfit and a hat filled with fruit on her head. Her sassy, playful attitude could be conveyed through her human features in a way that a plain old banana simply couldn't. By anthropomorphizing their logo, Chiquita could connect and communicate with their customers while building a powerhouse brand identity. In fact, Miss Chiquita represented the company for more than five decades; eventually the logo morphed from a banana into an actual woman in 1987.

Advertising characters aren't the only food-related creepy-cuties out there. Since the early 1950s, children across the globe have been laughing themselves silly over the crazy faces they've created for Mr. Potato Head. I was never a Mr. Potato Head kid. For all of my love of things anthropomorphic, he is the one I find creepy. Millions of people disagree with me, however, and count Mr. Potato Head among their most beloved childhood toys. Mid-century kids started gleefully sticking eyes, noses, mustaches, and more, first on actual potatoes, and then on plastic ones after the US government called foul on health regulations for encouraging the use of real vegetables, insisting that the manufacturer include a plastic potato designed for play. Many of my friends had a Mr. Potato Head when I was growing up. Those who had older siblings or cousins to bequeath them '60s-era

hand-me-down toys even had some of his weirdo friends like Willy Burger, Cooky Cucumber, or Oscar the Orange.

I was having none of it then, and I'm still having none of it. I never bought a Mr. Potato Head for my daughter, and she never asked for one. When I enquire as to whether or not she'd like one or ever wished she had one, I'm met with an emphatic *no*, in the tone she typically reserves for my more offensive questions. Perhaps our mutual dislike for creepy Mr. Potato Head is genetic. In any case, we both agree: give us a rubber-faced lady monkey doll any day.

In my experience, it's anthropomorphized animals that tend to elicit the most extreme reaction—especially the ones that that are simultaneously creepy and cute. Case in point: my vintage rubber-faced lady monkey toy called, appropriately enough, Monkey Lady.

Monkey Lady is a 1960-something toy with a stuffed cotton body, a rubber face and hands, and a thatch of fake fur atop her head. She carries a rubber banana that can be stuffed into her mouth. She looks jolly and adorable with her flowery calico-print stuffed body and removable yellow overskirt. So far, so cute. But then there's that pliable plastic face, all shifty eyes and poised lips, ready to whisper a secret or suck on the banana protruding from her right hand. Her expression isn't sinister, it's creepy, pure and simple.

Monchhichi Bebichhichi plush, China, 2011, ©Sekiguchi

Hello, Cutie!

There's something about Monkey Lady and her ilk that draws us in. Even those visitors to my home who think she's the most frightening thing they've ever seen cannot identify what makes her creepy. The same goes for those who find her really cute. Whenever I ask someone why they think Monkey Lady is creepy—or cute—I get but one answer, usually along the lines of "I don't know—she/it just *is*."

Monkeys are understandably one of the most popular animals to anthropomorphize, as we already share many traits with them. From sock monkeys to Zippy to Monchhichi, monkey toys have long been the perfect ambassadors of creepy-cute, and everyone's got an opinion. I decide that it's time to take a closer look at these three monkeys before I declare my personal verdict.

I have never owned a sock monkey. Somehow, this enduring icon of DIY crafts has never made it into my home, though not for a lack of trying on the part of my daughter, who loves them. Whenever we see them at the cool-stuff store up the street, she asks for one, and every time I say no. I'm not going to spend twenty-five dollars on a sock toy we could make at home (and then never do). But many, many people have. Popularized during the Great Depression, the toys were made of worn brown or grey socks with bright red heels that, when sewn, became the monkey's mouth.

Today, the sock monkey is enjoying a come-back, its likeness popping up on everything from knitted winter hats to Easter baskets. Renewed interest in the toys may well have been spurred by the success of designer Paul Frank, whose Julius the Monkey logo is reminiscent of the classic toy and has been gracing wallets, T-shirts, and pretty much everything else under the sun since its inception in 1995. My vote on the sock monkey: cute, but not for twenty-five dollars.

Zippy the Chimp, on the other hand, was an actual monkey who first appeared on *The Howdy Doody Show* and went on to make numerous other television appearances, most notably on *The Ed Sullivan Show*. From the 1950s through the '80s, various versions of Zippy dolls were produced, and original ones, dressed in Zippy's signature T-shirt and coveralls, which were manufactured by the Rushton Company, can fetch top prices online and in collectibles shops. I, however, will not be one of the collectors shelling out for a Zippy doll any time soon. There's something unsettling about Zippy. Unlike my beloved Monkey Lady's mischievous expression, Zippy's rubber face seems aggressive, maybe even mean. My vote: creepy.

Finally, there's Monchhichi. I can still hear the lyrics of the '80s television commercial in my head: "Monchhichi, Monchhichi, oh so soft and cuddly..." Hailing from Japan, the dolls have furry bodies and plastic heads, hands

Elephant squeaky toy, 1980s

Hello, Cutie!

and feet, and often hold a baby bottle. Monch-hichis' look is a brazen play for the hearts (and wallets) of cute collectors, and since the toy's introduction in Japan in 1974, it's worked.

Monchhichi didn't hit the big-time in North America until the 1980s when the brand was licensed to Mattel and an animated Hanna-Barbera television show hit the airwaves. I didn't have a Monchhichi when I was younger, but the image of the cute little monkey always stuck with me (along with the television jingle, it seems), so when in my mid-twenties I came across one at a Toronto shop specializing in vintage toys, I snapped it up immediately and tossed it into my handbag.

Later, at a social function, I had to dig around in my bag to find a business card and my new Monchhichi tumbled out onto the table. There was the dreaded moment of silence, and then one of my colleagues turned the doll right-side up and propped it against the wall. "It's so cute," said the woman I was attempting to find a business card for. "What is it?" asked one of the men in the group. I told them it was a Monchhichi, but was met with blank stares. "It's from Japan," I explained. Everyone nodded in understanding, and Monchhichi became our mascot for the night. Monchhichi? I vote super-cute.

Anthropomorphic toy animals like Mon-chhichi don't have the creepy-cute market cornered by any means. To me, it's real, live animals that have been crossing the line from cute to creepy recently. While Cute Overload is the champion of cute animal pictures, other niche websites and businesses have spun off on cute-animal tangents of their own. The group behind the site *I Can Has Cheezburger* have been slapping captions on animal photos since 2007 and are responsible for introducing the world to lolcats, which are photos of cats in silly situations with captions written in bad English and block letters.

Cats, in particular, seem to be subject to more creepy-cutesploitation than any other household pet, and it's the habit of dressing cats in costume that has had me on the creepy-cute fence lately. Through the years, I've had a lot of different books grace my coffee table, and I've come to notice that some get picked up by more guests to my home than others. But none have proved more irresistible than the 2011 book *Fashion Cats* by Takako Iwasa. Japan's self-proclaimed cat couturier, Iwasa makes her living crafting outfits for felines, including a bridal ensemble, a Hogwarts-esque hat, cape, and tie set, and a "Hello Kitty Transformation Kit," so your real cat can dress up like a fake one. I'm torn. The pictures are cute, but then I remember, *that's a live cat*, and I start to wonder how anyone could get a cat to wear a costume, let alone sit still and pose for a picture in one, and that's where things get creepy for me.

Back in the 1980s, Japanese photographer Satoru Tsuda made a name for himself and his Perlorian Cats by dressing up the animals and placing them in elaborate dioramas. Tsuda's cat kitsch even made it onto the cover of *Artforum* magazine in 1986. But in the late '80s, accusations of drugging were raised—though never proved—as animal rights groups took the photographer to task. The cats quietly faded away, but have been inching toward a comeback in the past few years.

Cats dressed in costumes: creepy or cute? Like so many aspects of cute culture, it could go either way—it's a matter of empathy and aesthetics. We all have internal radar that registers the creepy and the cute, and more and more the two overlap. There are artists and manufacturers who purposefully set out to mix the creepy with the cute, and the aesthetic is continually evolving into new and inspired toys, crafts, clothing, and more. This evolution makes cute-hunting an adventure, filled with curious what-on-earth-is-that moments and great friends. The subjectivity of cute—or creepy, or creepy-cute—results in a never-ending conversation, complete with disagreement, laughter, and thoughtful debate because, like beauty, what is cute truly is in the eye of the beholder.

Hello, Cutie!

Cute Goes Rogue

ARTIST MEGHAN MURPHY POKES GENTLE FUN AT CUTE CULTURE

Meghan Murphy

Photo: Meghan Murphy

"It's like Hello Kitty off her meds. Or sparkly insanity. Or a cloud that craps rainbows." This is how Meghan Murphy describes her web comic, Kawaii Not, and her summary couldn't be more apt. If you've yet to see *kawaiinot.com* or either of Meghan's books, *Kawaii Not: Cute Gone Bad* or *Kawaii Not, Too: Cute Gets Badder,* you're missing out on some harmless, satirical fun. The short strips are illustrated in a style familiar to all cute enthusiasts and draws heavily upon the super-cutesy Japanese aesthetic that typically involves slapping a smiling face on everything from fruit to cameras.

Meghan's humor is juvenile and silly, but never nasty or mean. In fact, she's a big fan of cute herself. "I honestly love cute/kawaii stuff," she says. "I am fascinated by its appeal, even when I don't fully understand it. Part of Kawaii Not has always been my attempt to explore the line between cute and naughty. Sometimes it's thinner than you think."

That thin line is where the funniest material lies. Case in point: one of the most popular Kawaii Not strips (and T-shirts) depicting a happy little knife that exclaims, "I feel a little bit stabbity today!" As Meghan points out, "Everyone has had at least one of those days filled with crappy people and dark thoughts. Instead of being alone, this comic says, 'It's okay; I've been there too.' And sometimes a smile is scarier than a blade."

Meghan, who is based in Rochester, New York, and works as a professional designer and illustrator, introduced Kawaii Not on LiveJournal in 2005. Since then, the little comic she dared herself to do has grown into a brand, complete with merchandise and a loyal legion of fans. Still, her fascination with cute culture endures, and the mystery of its allure is one of the key factors that keep Kawaii Not going. "I don't think I'll ever completely understand kawaii culture, but then again, I don't think anyone can," she says. "It's complex, and means different things to different people. There is something deep in the human brain that responds to cute, some primordial attraction to big eyes and wide smiles."

One thing that she does understand is the symbiosis between kawaii and the Internet. "Perhaps it's the semi-anonymity [people have] online that allows them to open up and embrace the cute, to feel safe enough to let down their walls and enjoy kittens and ponies and rainbows, and share some un-ironic enjoyment with others."

Meghan Murphy's webcomic, *Kawaii Not*.
Photo: Meghan Murphy

Artwork by *Kawaii Not* creator, Meghan Murphy.
Photo: Meghan Murphy

kawaiinot.com
murphypop.com
Twitter: @kawaiinot
Shop: kawaiinot.bigcartel.com/
Tumblr: murphypop.tumblr.com/
Facebook: facebook.com/pages/Kawaii-Not/
   115814542860
DeviantArt: medox.deviantart.com/

Hello, Cutie!

Haunting Beauty

ARTIST MAB GRAVES' "GIRLS" EVOKE BOTH CREEPY AND CUTE

Mab Graves

Photo: Larry Endicott

I have a confession to make: I am totally, completely, 100 percent in love with Mab Graves' art. I own a small, doll-sized locket featuring a hand-painted peppermint candy with a face and a rather serious expression. I want more than almost anything one of her custom Blythe dolls and a painting for my living room. Her work screams dark fairy tale to me, and I couldn't be more pleased to hear that Mab does indeed take much of her inspiration from those old Grimms' tales. As she says of the fictional girls she paints on canvas and lockets and prints on cards, "They all have old souls and a somber 'knowingness.'" That's not to say the girls aren't cute.

Mab's work has attracted an impressive following. Her dark-cute combo certainly strikes a chord in those of us who don't want our cute all sweet, all the time. "I think it is so interesting because not everyone gets it," Mab says of her style. "It takes a sharp wit and a keen sense of irony to be able to appreciate. It's like a secret club. When you meet someone and they 'get' it there is an instant camaraderie—like an inside joke that the rest of the population is simply not wired to understand."

There are, however, enough people who are wired to understand her aesthetic to keep the Indianapolis-based artist more than busy and motivated. She's one of those people who can see artistic potential in the seemingly mundane. "I have never, in my entire life, been bored. I have always had a cacophony of images swirling about in my head kinetically jingling about waiting to be brought to life," Mab says of her artistic process and the everyday items and experiences that influence her wondrous, surreal work. "When I look up at things, or just glance in passing at unfamiliar objects, my mind identifies them as some utterly fantastical thing. Then, of course, I look again and they have sneakily morphed into a hat stand or a lump of cement. I 'see' my paintings everywhere, hiding in ordinary objects."

Mab's work is anything but ordinary, and there's always an expected twist lurking in her images, whether it's the attitude portrayed on a greeting card by Genevieve, a girl clutching a pet unicorn, or the vicious snarl of the cat held by green-masked Scarlett Madcat. Mab describes her style as "Grimmsical"—both Grimm (as in the fairy-tale brothers) and whimsical. "I try very hard to maintain a subtle balance between the cute and creepy," she says. "This is very important because it's a slippery slope and it's all too easy to take things too far. When I am in a gallery and I have someone come up to me and say, 'There's something that totally weirds me out about that piece, but I just can't put my finger on it,' I know I have done my job."

. . . .

www.mabgraves.com
Shop: etsy.com/shop/mabgraves
Blog: mabgraves.blogspot.com/
Facebook: facebook.com/mab.graves
Flickr: flickr.com/photos/mabgraves/
Pinterest: pinterest.com/mabgraves/

"Tuesday and Wednesday Addams—the Addams Twins," an original cameo painting by Mab Graves. Photo: Mab Graves

Emiko: a Mab Girl, custom Blythe doll by Mab Graves. Photo: Mab Graves

Epilogue

There is a point, inevitably, in the writing of any book in which the writer begins to suffer from fatigue. That fatigue often rolls into self-doubt and sometimes even into a brief but deep loathing of the subject matter. Thankfully, any fatigue and self-doubt I experienced while researching, writing, and photographing this book did not result in any loathing whatsoever. How could it? Everything, it seemed, about putting this project together was as cute as can be.

I believed at the onset that I knew a fair bit about cute culture and its inhabitants, but was quickly humbled by the expertise of others—and inspired by their enthusiasm. I learned that cute culture wasn't just about mere stuff; it was also about the people who love and collect it. Cute hunters run the gamut from doll collectors to clown aficionados, from My Little Pony devotees and those hooked on Strawberry Shortcake to people obsessed with Japan and all things kawaii. But whatever their personal niche, they all have one thing in common: an unabashed passion for their hobby.

It's this passion that egged me on through the writing of this book. The connections I made and conversations I had put a smile on my face every day. Entering more deeply into the cute community than I had before, I was surprised and delighted by the number of like-minded individuals I encountered and their willingness to share their stories and experiences. Cute, in turn, has taken on new meaning and depth for me.

I don't feel as silly about naming my Blythe dolls and assigning them all distinct personalities; I no longer feel weird making up elaborate stories about the "lives" of my kitschy ceramic dogs, Mr Chuff and Lovey. I understand that it's perfectly natural to feel empathy for objects, particularly ones with typically cute features, and I have no desire to return to the pre-*Hello, Cutie!* days when I frequently felt that it was just me, my daughter, and a handful of far-flung friends against the cold, hard, and decidedly un-cute world.

On its surface, cute culture may seem whimsical, perhaps even absurd. That cute culture exists at all is surely enough to have cynics scoffing. But I can meet every critical tut-tut with a secret smile because the joy that cute brings to the lives of its fans is immeasurable. Until I researched and wrote this book, I hadn't given much thought to just how much my cute collections have calmed and comforted me during difficult times. There's no shame in turning to objects to help us cope, nor is it wrong to openly toast cute and honor its contribution to our lives.

The time is long overdue for cute to be celebrated. The Sloan song "If It Feels Good Do It" plays in my head as I glance around my living room, taking a moment to look at the cute objects scattered about. My gaze settles on the Creature, my made-in-Japan baby squeaky bear that no longer squeaks, my oldest cute friend. He doesn't speak, of course, or move, or do anything supernatural, but I like to think there's something behind those big, hand-painted eyes. Carry on, I imagine him saying, carry on.

About the Contributors

Photo: Elle Mohan

Katie Barker

Etsy: poshtottydesignz.etsy.com
Folksy: folksy.com/shops/poshtottydesignz
Flickr: flickr.com/photos/40731889@N08/
  sets/72157622600035056/

Photo: Julia Chibatbar

Julia Chibatar

Etsy: ghostgap.etsy.com
Etsy: angelsandcrafts.etsy.com
Twitter: @ghostgap
Facebook: facebook.com/pages/Ghostgap/
  122796167822771
Flickr: flickr.com/photos/ghostgap/

Photo: Megan Besmirched

Megan Besmirched

besmirched.com
saltydame.com
Twitter: @besmirched
Facebook: facebook.com/meganbesmirched
Etsy: etsy.com/shop/besmirched

Photo: Anna Collver

Anna Collver

Blog: annasponies.blogspot.com/
Flickr: flickr.com/photos/aquamaeanna/
  collections/72157594587120722/

Photo: Pamela Klaffke

Kimberly Cook
Twitter: @maidencanada76
Facebook: facebook.com/GLTRGRRL
Flickr: flickr.com/photos/smittenkitten1976/

Photo: Alexandra Tyler

Leslie Dotson Van Every
modernkiddo.com

Photo: Sara Doane

Sara Doane
Etsy: etsy.com/shop/Agent137
Blog: agent137.blogspot.com/

Photo: School Portrait Studios

Cynthia Flores
LiveJournal: ggsdolls.livejournal.com/
Blog: ggsdolls.blogspot.com/
Etsy: etsy.com/shop/ggsdolls

Hello, Cutie!

Patrick W. Galbraith
kodanshausa.com/
books/9784770031013/

Mab Graves
mabgraves.com/
Shop: etsy.com/shop/mabgraves
Blog: mabgraves.blogspot.com/
Facebook: facebook.com/mab.graves
Flickr: flickr.com/photos/mabgraves/
Pinterest: pinterest.com/mabgraves/

Gina Garan
thisisblythe.com

Shimrit Hamsi
shimrita.blogspot.com
Etsy: shimrita.etsy.com
Facebook: facebook.com
  /#!/pages/Shimritas-Cup
  cakes/175112220941

Faythe Levine

faythelevine.com
skyhighmilwaukee.com
signpaintermovie.com
handmadenationmovie.com
artvscraftmke.com
Twitter: @faythelevine

Toni Morberg

buttercreambakeshoppe.com
Facebook: facebook.com/#!/
  buttercreambakeshoppe

Rosanna Mackney

tofucute.com
Twitter: @tofu_cute
Facebook: facebook.com/tofucute
Flickr: flickr.com/tofu_cute

Missy Munday

Etsy: etsy.com/shop/boopsiedaisy
Flickr: flickr.com/photos/boopsiedaisy/
Blog: boopsiedaisy.blogspot.ca/

Hello, Cutie!

Photo: Meghan Murphy

Meghan Murphy

kawaiinot.com | murphypop.com
Twitter: @kawaiinot
Shop: kawaiinot.bigcartel.com/
Tumblr: murphypop.tumblr.com/
Facebook: facebook.com/pages/Kawaii-Not/
  115814542860
DeviantArt: medox.deviantart.com/

Photo: : Thomas Pierrepont

Jane Pierrepont

pollymakes.co.uk
Etsy: etsy.com/shop/polly
Etsy: etsy.com/shop/jollypolly
Flickr: flickr.com/photos/polly-jane

Photo: Pamela Klaffke

Naomi Owen

Twitter: @agentowen
Flickr: flickr.com/photos/weeping_sabicu/

Photo: ©Momiji

Claire Rowlands

lovemomiji.com
Facebook: facebook.com/momijihq
Twitter: @momijihq
Pintrest: pinterest.com/MomijiHQ/
Instagram: @momijihq

Photo: Michael Canterino

Crystal Scott
crystalfaithscott.com
girlclownfilm.com
Facebook: crystalfaithscottfanpage
Facebook: facebook.com/girlclownfilm
Twitter: @crystalscott
Twitter: @girlclownfilm

Photo: Alexandra Tyler

Alexandra Tyler
Blog: modernkiddo.com
Twitter: @galexina
Instagram: @galexina

Photo: © Flash Photo

Susan Wilson
www.irocf.org

Photo: Kayla Lukes

Victoria Suzanne
parfaitdoll.com
Twitter: @victoriasuzanne
Tumblr: angel-cake.tumblr.com/
Instagram: victoriasuzanne

Photo: Stefanie Sakamoto

Crystal Watanabe
Blog: fictionalfood.net
Blog: www.aibento.net
Twitter: @pikko

Photo: Roz Boatman

Fanny Zara
Blog: blythe-doll-fashions.com/
Flickr: flickr.com/photos/
   mademoiselleblythe/
Facebook: facebook.com/
   fanny.zara
Twitter: @fannyzara

Hello, Cutie!

Select Bibliography

Anderton, Johana Gast. *More Twentieth Century Dolls: From Bisque to Vinyl.* Des Moines: Wallace Homestead, 1974.

Anonymous. "Land of the Rising Fun." *The Wilson Quarterly* 34, no. 1 (2010).

Avella, Natalie. *Graphic Japan: From Woodblock and Zen to Manga and Kawaii.* Mies [u.a.]: Rotovision, 2004.

Belson, Ken and Brian Bremner. *Hello Kitty: The Remarkable Story of Sanrio and the Billion Dollar Feline Phenomenon.* Singapore: John Wiley & Sons Asia, 2004.

Belluz, Julia. "What You Need Is a Beautiful Bento Lunch: A Japanese Food Writer Offers Up Recipes for Aesthetically Arranged Meals-in-a-Box." *Maclean's* (January 31, 2011).

Black, Rosemary. "Why Kids Collect." *Parents* (July 1995).

Chozick, Amy. "Culture: The Cool Factory; How Japan Made Hip a Business." *Wall Street Journal Asia* (March 16, 2007).

Cope, Peter and Dawn Cope. *Dean's Rag Books and Rag Dolls.* London: New Cavendish, 2009.

Craig, Timothy J., ed. *Japan Pop: Inside the World of Japanese Pop Culture.* New York: East Gate Books, 2000.

Cross, Gary. *Kids' Stuff: Toys and the Changing World of American Childhood.* Cambridge, MA: Harvard University Press.

DeLapp, Richard. *Pictorial Encyclopedia of Japanese Culture: The Soul and Heritage of Japan.* Tokyo: Gakken, 1987.

Francke, Tyler. "Kewpie Lovers Unite For Annual Branson Festival." *Branson Tri-Lakes News* (April 19, 2011).

Fujita, Yuiko. "Fabricating Japaneseness? The Identity Politics of Young Designers and Artists in Global Cities." *International Journal of Japanese Sociology* 20, no. 1 (2011).

Garger, Ilya. "One Nation Under Cute." *Psychology Today* (March/April 2007).

Gerbert, Elaine. "Dolls in Japan." *The Journal of Popular Culture* 35, no. 3 (2001).

Gibbs, Mark. "Hacking the Cuteness Out of Furby." *Network World* (December 4, 2000).

Harris, Daniel. *Cute, Quaint, Hungry and Romantic: The Aesthetics of Consumerism.* New York: Da Capo Press, 2001.

Holland, Thomas W., ed. *Girls' Toys of the Fifties and Sixties: Memorable Catalog Pages From the Legendary Sears Christmas Wishbooks 1950–1969.* Sherman Oaks, CA: Windmill Press, 1997.

Howes, Carol. "Don't Get Mad, Get Even: Reprogram Furby: Hacking Kit on Net Lets You Mess With Chatty Toy." *National Post* (January 6, 2001).

Ito, Kinko. "A History of Manga In the Context of Japanese Culture and Society." *The Journal of Popular Culture* 38, no. 3.

Khaleel, Homa. "Mummy, Can I Have Miss Piggy For Lunch Today?" *The Guardian* (January 2012).

La Rocco, Claudia. "Hello Creepy: A Spooky Side to Japan's Cute Culture." *New York Times* (January 13, 2010).

Lorenz, Konrad. *Studies in Animal and Human Behavior*, Vol. 2. Cambridge, MA: Harvard University Press, 1971.

Matsumaru, Kumi. "The Doe-Eyed World of Makoto Takahashi." *Daily Yomiuri* (June 10, 2010).

Meikle, Jeffery L. *American Plastic: A Cultural History*. New Brunswick, NJ: Rutgers University Press, 1995.

Miller, Laura. "Cute Masquerade and the Pimping of Japan." *International Journal of Japanese Sociology* 20, no. 1, (2011).

Morreall, John. "Cuteness." *British Journal of Aesthetics* 31, no. 1 (1991).

Muensterberger, Werner. *Collecting: An Unruly Passion—Psychological Perspectives*. New York: Harcourt Brace & Company, 1995.

Ngai, Sianne, S. "The Cuteness of the Avant-Garde." *Critical Inquiry* 31, no. 4 (2005).

Noxon, Christopher. *Rejuvenile: Kickball, Cartoons, Cupcakes and the Reinvention of the American Grown-Up*. New York: Crown, 2006.

Panati, Charles. *Panati's Parade of Fads, Follies and Mania: The Origins of Our Cherished Obsessions*. New York: HarperPerennial, 1991.

Phoenix, Woodrow. *Plastic Culture: How Japanese Toys Conquered the World*. Tokyo: Kodansha, 2006.

Pincott, Jena. "Pretty Young Things: Does Cuteness Last?" *Psychology Today* (November 2011).

Queenan, Joe. "Time For a Frosty Farewell to Cupcakes." *Wall Street Journal* (May 21, 2011).

Robinson-Escriout, Roxanne. "Blythe Spirit." *Women's Wear Daily* (May 2002).

Salmans, Sandra. "Little Miss Was Born to Sell." *New York Times* (February 10, 1981).

Sanders, John. "On 'Cuteness'." *British Journal of Aesthetics* 32, no. 2 (1992).

Scott, Sharon M. *Toys and American Culture: An Encyclopedia*. Santa Barbara, CA: Greenwood, 2010.

Hello, Cutie!

Skov, Lise and Brian Moeran. *Women, Media and Consumption In Japan*. Honolulu: University of Hawai'i Press, 1996.

Shono, Kazumichi. "Little Giants of Business: World Leader in Funny Erasers Cranks Out 150,000 a Day." *The Daily Yomiuri* (November 1, 2010).

Smith, Louvinia T. "Kewpie Dolls." *Antiques & Collecting Magazine* (April 1999).

Spindler, Amy M. "Do You Otaku?" *New York Times Magazine* (February 2002).

Storey, Samantha. "Bento Boxes Win Lunch Fans." *New York Times* (September 9, 2009).

Suttisiltum, Samila. "Blythe Mania; Meet the Wide-Eyed Little Miss Who's Stealing the Hearts of Bangkok's Most Stylish Citizens." *Bangkok Post* (May 18, 2008).

Tabuchi, Hiroko. "In Search of Adorable, as Hello Kitty Gets Closer to Goodbye." *New York Times* (May 14, 2010).

Trucco, Terry. "In Japan, Cuteness Counts." *Wall Street Journal* (February 21, 1986).

Tucker, Patrick. "Survival of the Cutest: 'Lovable' May Be the Most Practical Evolutionary Trait For Endangered Species." *The Futurist* (May–June 2007).

Whymant, Robert. "Japan Goes Walkies With Its Virtual Pets." *The Times* (January 23, 1997).

Wilkes, David. "Cupcake Calamity: Website Discount Deal Leaves Baker Swamped By Orders For 102,000 Cakes and Wipes Out Her Profits" *Daily Mail* (November 22, 2011).

Windolf, Jim. "Addicted to Cute." *Vanity Fair* (December 2009).

Yano, Christine. "Wink on Pink: Interpreting Japanese Cute as It Grabs the Global Headlines." *The Journal of Asian Studies* 68, no. 3 (2009).

Index

Note: Page numbers in italics indicate photographs.

PAMELA KLAFFKE is a newspaper and magazine journalist turned novelist and photographer. She is the author of the non-fiction book *Spree: A Cultural History of Shopping* and the novels *Snapped* and *Every Little Thing*. She lives in Calgary, Canada, with her fiancé, philosopher Gillman Payette, and her daughter.